A Genealogist's Guide to

DISCOVERING YOUR
Italian
ANCESTORS

How to find and record your unique heritage

Lynn Nelson

BETTERWAY BOOKS
CINCINNATI, OHIO

Other fine Betterway Books are available from your local bookstore or direct from the publisher.

01   00   99   98   97   5   4   3   2   1

Library of Congress Cataloging-in-Publication Data

Nelson, Lynn.
    A genealogist's guide to discovering your Italian ancestors / Lynn Nelson.—1st ed.
        p.   cm.
    Includes bibliographical references and index.
    ISBN 1-55870-426-4 (alk. paper)
    1. Italy—Genealogy—Handbooks, manuals, etc. 2. Italian-Americans—Genealogy—
    Handbooks, manuals, etc. I. Title.
CS753.N45   1997
929'.1'072045—dc21   97-8280
                                                                                   CIP

Edited by Argie J. Manolis
Production Edited by Michelle Kramer
Designed by Angela Lennert Wilcox
Cover photo provided courtesy of the Ambrose/Neroni family

Some material in this publication is reprinted by permission of The Church of Jesus Christ of Latter-day Saints. In granting permission for this use of copyrighted material, the Church does not imply or express either endorsement or authorization of this publication.

Betterway Books are available for sales promotions, premiums and fund-raising use. Special editions or book excerpts can also be created to specification. For details contact: Special Sales Manager, F&W Publications, 1507 Dana Avenue, Cincinnati, Ohio 45207.

ABOUT THE AUTHOR

Lynn Nelson has been successfully researching her Italian heritage for many years and speaks at genealogy conferences on this, her favorite subject. She holds a bachelor's degree in psychology from the State University of New York at Stony Brook. Currently, Lynn works as a computer programmer/analyst and is the author of two techincal computer books. She lives in rural Maryland, from where, she says, it is even possible to research Italian records.

ACKNOWLEDGMENTS

The author wishes to thank the staff of The Family History Library of the Church of Jesus Christ of Latter-day Saints and particularly, the staff at the Family History Center in Lancaster, Pennsylvania. Without their resources, this book would not be possible.

To my immigrant ancestors:

Pasquale Luisi & Rosa Quartodipalo

Vincenzo Nano & Rosa Lamberti

Table of Contents

SECTION I **INTRODUCTION**

CHAPTER ONE
Ancestor Hunting in the Boot ... 2

Returning to Your Roots

CHAPTER TWO
How to Use This Book ... 4

Overview
Your Research Process
Summary of Steps for Italian Research

SECTION II **BACKGROUND**

CHAPTER THREE
Some General Genealogical Guidelines ... 7

Always Have a Specific Goal
Understanding Cluster Genealogy
Record Keeping
Confirming Information
For More Information

CHAPTER FOUR
History of Italy for the Genealogist ... 10

Before 1796
1796-1815
1815-1860
1860-1870
The Tie Between History and Genealogy
Geographical Organization of Italy
Italian Naming Traditions and
  Their Ramifications
Nineteenth-Century Italian Society

CHAPTER FIVE
Determining Your Immigrant Ancestor's Hometown ... 22

Italian Immigration to North America
North American Resources
Name Changes
The Basic Facts Required
Primary Versus Secondary Sources
Interviews With Family and Friends
Primary Sources
Secondary American Resources
Italian Resources

SECTION III **THE RECORDS**

CHAPTER SIX
Stato Civile: *Vital Records* ... 34

Some Disadvantages and
  How to Overcome Them
Advantages of the *Stato Civile*

CHAPTER SEVEN
The Best Tips for Using the Stato Civile ... 37

Old Style Handwriting
Abbreviations
Word Continuations
Interpreting Colloquialisms and Idioms
Utilizing the Indices
Example of Birth Record Index
Example of Marriage Record Index
Example of Death Record Index
Read Those Margin Notations
Taking Advantage of Redundancy
Secrets of Using an Italian/English Dictionary

CHAPTER EIGHT

The Records ... 53

Atto di Nascita—Birth Record
Marriage Records
Atto di Matrimonio—Marriage Record
Processetti
Atto di Morte—Death Record

CHAPTER NINE

Where to Find the Records ... 81

The Family History Library
Research by Correspondence

SECTION IV **A CASE STUDY**

CHAPTER TEN

Searching for Francesco; a Step-by-Step Example ... 90

SECTION V **CONCLUSIONS**

CHAPTER ELEVEN

Other Research Options ... 114

Some Interesting Miscellaneous Research
Where to Go From Here

APPENDICES

APPENDIX A

Italian Word Lists ... 117

APPENDIX B

Italian Letter-Writing Guide ... 123

APPENDIX C

Addresses of the Italian Archives ... 128

APPENDIX D

Research Forms ... 137

Bibliography ... 142

Index ... 144

FOREWORD

Wouldn't you love to have a professional genealogist by your side when you're climbing your family tree? A genealogist experienced in Italian research who would lead you step-by-step through the process of finding your ancestors, warning you of potential problems, sharing valuable tips and answering your questions along the way? What a great companion!

Well, you're holding that companion in your hands right now! This book is the next best thing to your own personal genealogist.

If you haven't yet pursued your Italian ancestors because you didn't know where to start, this book will get you started. If you are reluctant to research Italian records because you think you can't read Italian, this book will show you that you *can* understand Italian documents. If you have hit a roadblock in your Italian research, this book will show you the detour.

Using the methods detailed in this book, you will be amazed and delighted to see how quickly and easily you can discover your Italian ancestors, without going abroad. You should have no trouble tracing ancestors back as far as the 1700s!

So what are you waiting for? Let's get started!

"For us to go to Italy and to penetrate into Italy is like a most fascinating act of self-discovery—back, back down the old ways of time. Strange and wonderful chords awake in us, and vibrate again after many hundreds of years of complete forgetfulness."

D.H. Lawrence, *Sea and Sardinia*, 1921.

SECTION I

Introduction

CHAPTER ONE

Ancestor Hunting in the Boot

Daylight faded as three young girls rushed through the streets of Rutigliano, Italy, on a late summer day in 1823. "Hurry or we'll be late," Giacoma Savino warned her cousin, Rosa, and her best friend, Carmina.

"Tomorrow you'll be Pasquale Nuzzi's wife, Giacoma!" teased Carmina. The girls giggled as they reached the steps of the town hall just as the church bells rang for eight o'clock. They sobered as they entered the building.

Pasquale looked up and smiled as his bride-to-be approached the mayor's desk. "Well," said Signóre Catelino to the young couple, "it looks like we're ready to record your marriage promise. Tomorrow is the big day!"

Vito Pappalardi trudged to the town hall for the third time this month. "July of 1837 will be remembered for the worst epidemic in the history of San Pietro," he said to his cousin, Nunzio. Last night their neighbor's son, three-year-old Vincenzo, was the latest victim.

They entered the cheerless building and waited in line behind several other townspeople. By the look on their faces, Vito knew they were here for the same reason as he.

Their turn came and they walked up to the clerk. "We're here to report a death," Vito said.

Francesco Lamberti carried his day-old son into Caserta's town hall. "Congratulations on your firstborn!" greeted mayor Valentino. Francesco proudly uncovered the *bambino*. "Look. He has my eyes," he beamed. "His name is Pietro, after my father."

Signoré Valentino smiled at the happy father as he wrote the birth record.

These are the stories of our ancestors found in the vital records of Italy. The marriages, deaths and births of our ancestors, recorded throughout the nineteenth century, are waiting to tell us their stories.

This book will take you on a quest into your past. You will meet your ancestors and discover your Italian heritage on this wonderful journey of history, culture, mystery, self-discovery and, of course, fun!

Returning to Your Roots

Interest in the pursuit of one's ancestors is ever-increasing. There are hundreds of thousands of fellow genealogists joining you in this hobby, many of them of Italian descent. Why all this interest in discovering dead relatives?

In our very mobile society where families are frequently separated by great distances, genealogy is a way to get back to family roots. Maybe discovering how our great-great-grandparents lived as extended families, with many generations under one roof, vicariously satisfies that need for closer family ties.

Others pursue genealogy like mystery fans grab the latest best-selling thriller, anxious to figure out "whodunit." Discovering your ancestors is a special mystery. It is challenging enough to maintain interest *and* it is very rewarding—an addictive combination. Best of all, the puzzle is never completely finished. Each time you solve the mystery for one branch of your family tree, a whole new branch sprouts.

Genealogy is a great hobby for collectors. Just like a coin collector searching for that elusive buffalo nickel, a genealogist hunts for great-great-grandmother Rosa's maiden name. Each newly discovered ancestor fills a space in the collection.

Italian genealogy is especially exciting because it is easier than that of most other nationalities. There is a great wealth of information available right here in North America, so you don't have to go abroad to discover your Italian roots.

In the pursuit of your Italian ancestors you will come to understand the history and culture of Italy, and with that, the motivations of your ancestors. Your ancestors become much more than faceless names—they become family.

So put on your detective's hat, grab your notebook and don't forget a handkerchief for those joyful reunions with your long lost ancestors. Let's begin ancestor hunting in the boot.

CHAPTER TWO

How to Use This Book

Overview

This is a practical, hands-on guide meant to be used frequently. First, read through it completely. During your research, you will find yourself referring back to different sections.

The focus of this book is using Italian vital records to climb your family tree. Vital records, the civil documents that record births, marriages and deaths, are the best place to start your research because they are readily available in the United States and Canada and are relatively easy to use. If you are a beginner in Italian research, this book will take you, step-by-step, through the research process. It also contains many advanced tips and techniques, useful to the more experienced researcher.

The rest of Section I, the Introduction, will describe this book and how to use it. Follow the recommended steps suggested here.

Section II, Background, covers some general guidelines that are critical to a successful genealogical research project. Using these rules will insure success. A brief history of Italy as it pertains to genealogy provides important and interesting information that will assist you in understanding and using Italian vital records. The last chapter in Section II shows how to determine the Italian hometown of your original Italian immigrant ancestor.

Section III, Using the Records, makes up the bulk of this book. An overview of Italian vital records, their advantages and disadvantages, prepares you for your research. Chapter seven, The Best Tips for Using Italian Records, is full of valuable advice. You will refer to this chapter again and again. The next chapter covers the actual vital records, discussing how each type of record was created and what information it contains. In this chapter, we will review actual record examples. This is where you will learn how to read these documents. The final chapter of

Section III shows you how to obtain the vital records of Italy.

Section IV provides a case study that illustrates the research process in a step-by-step fashion, from determining a research objective to finding and interpreting actual vital records. Follow this example to understand how to perform your own research.

The last section will provide references and offer suggestions on where to go to continue your research beyond the existence of the vital records.

The appendices contain more valuable reference information. Italian word lists, containing most of the words that you will encounter in the vital records, will aid you in translations. A letter-writing guide will assist you in obtaining information from Italy when you need to resort to that tactic. Finally, special forms are provided to assist you with your research. You may make copies of these forms for your own use.

Your Research Process

The actual vital records that you will use in your research originated in the town where the event occurred, so you must know the name of that town to find these records. If you haven't yet identified the Italian hometown of your original immigrant ancestor, read the Background section, particularly chapter five (Determining Your Immigrant Ancestor's Hometown) which will show you the necessary steps to discover that information. Once you have learned the name of that Italian town, then the rest of this book will guide you through your research. If you already know the Italian town, follow the step-by-step instructions listed below to begin your research.

This book contains many examples of actual Italian documents, each appearing in four formats: original, transcribed, translated and extracted.

The original format shows the actual document. It is in Italian and includes the handwritten sections. The transcribed format replaces the handwritten Italian script with typed Italian script. Comparing this to the original will assist you in understanding and learning the frequently unusual nineteenth-century handwriting. The translated format is typed English text showing how the document translates from Italian to English. Use this format to assist in translating documents from Italian to English. The extracted format simply shows the important genea-logical information from the document on a stan-dard form, which illustrates how to use the Data Extract Forms from this book. Study these examples carefully and frequently before you do your own research and you will quickly learn to read and un-derstand Italian vital records.

Most of your research involves using microfilm at your local Family History Center. If you have never visited a Family History Center before, or don't even know what one is, don't worry. Chapter nine will introduce you to this wonderful resource.

When you find your very first Italian record, oth-ers will quickly follow. By following the techniques described in this guide, your Italian family tree will quickly sprout with many branches. Once you suc-

---

Summary of Steps for Italian Research

1. Read this guide completely.
2. Determine your immigrant ancestor's hometown (see Chapter five).
3. Establish a specific research goal (see Chapter three).
4. Determine where the information is located (see Chapter nine).
5. Perform the research. You will refer back to this book again and again for tips, techniques and examples.
6. Repeat steps three through five for each new research goal.

---

ceed in meeting your first research goal, you will have some new information from which you can establish another research goal. This process can continue until you have exhausted the vital records.

The list of steps in the sidebar above outlines how to successfully climb your Italian family tree. Appendix C contains a more detailed checklist of this outline that you may copy. Use one form for each research objective.

Background

CHAPTER THREE

Some General Genealogical Guidelines

Before we get to the Italian vital records, it is very important to review some general genealogical research guidelines. These guidelines apply not just to Italian research but to all genealogical research. Entire books have been written about this topic, so I will only attempt to mention a few points that are essential for success. At the end of this chapter are references to several good books that cover this subject in depth.

Always Have a Specific Goal

This rule is most important. Every time you do genealogical research it is critical that you have a specific goal. Too many people just wander into a Family History Center thinking, "I'll just look for the name Luisi in Bari, Italy, and see what I can find." Even if they do find some listings of Luisi, have they discovered their ancestors? Maybe or maybe not. There is no way to know because the original research goal was too vague.

The goal must be focused. For example, "I want to find the birth record of my great-great-grandfather Pasquale Luisi who was born in Bari, Italy, in 1868." This research goal is specific enough to promise success.

A good method of testing whether your research goals are specific is the four *W*s: who, what, where and when.

- **Who** are you looking for? Pasquale Luisi
- **What** are you looking for? His birth record
- **Where** was the record created? Bari, Italy
- **When** was the record created? In 1868

If you can answer all four *W*s, your research goal is specific enough. If you are missing the answer to even one of the four *W*s, you are jumping ahead of yourself in your research. In that case you must take a step back and establish a goal that will help you answer the missing *W*.

If we know who, what and where, but we don't know when, we should first create a research goal to determine when. If we don't know in which year Pasquale was born, we would establish a goal to answer that question. Maybe we could find a document that lists his age, from which we can calculate a birth year. For example, if we know that he lived in New York City in 1920, we could try to find his census record which will show his age. So our research goal would be:

- Who: Pasquale Luisi
- What: Census record
- Where: New York City
- When: 1920

Once we find this record, we can calculate his birth year, plug that answer into the missing *W*, and we can move on to our next research goal. Each successful research session provides us with answers to more of the four *W*s, from which we can create new research goals.

Using this method to do genealogical research, I have had over 95 percent success in finding the records I want. The less than 5 percent failure rate is usually due to my making assumptions when answering the four *W*s.

The Four *W*s method helps focus on and find specific ancestors. However, once you have found that ancestor on a particular microfilm, you may want to review that film for other ancestors, bringing us to the next important point.

Understanding Cluster Genealogy

Cluster genealogy involves researching not only your direct ancestors, but their brothers, sisters, cousins, etc. Too many beginners focus exclusively on their direct ancestors and completely ignore the others, which can be a mistake.

Studying the family cluster is important for several reasons. First, it is more interesting to have knowledge about the whole family. Seen as a whole, they develop personalities instead of being just a list of names and dates.

Knowing about the siblings may also help you in the research of your direct ancestors. For example, you wish to find the marriage record of your fourth great-grandparents but you're not sure of their exact marriage year. You only know that they were married before 1836 because their daughter (your third great-grandmother) was born in mid-1836. You could just start looking through all the years from 1835 and earlier, but this could take a long time, especially if those years span several microfilms.

If you have been collecting information about the siblings of your third great-grandmother, however, this task might be easier. For example, you know that your third great-grandmother had at least four older siblings, the first born in 1829. You could then narrow the date range for the marriage of their parents to the years prior to 1829 and save a lot of time that you would have wasted in searching the years between 1829 and 1835.

If you hit a roadblock while researching your direct ancestor, you may be able to research the siblings instead since they share the same parents. For example, the records for the birth year of your great-great-grandfather, Domenico, are missing (maybe they were destroyed by a flood or are just simply lost). If you know of his siblings, you could pursue their birth records instead and still learn about Domenico's parents.

So don't ignore the relatives of your direct ancestor because they could be the key to success in your research. The way Italian vital records are organized and indexed makes this task very easy. You will learn more about this in a later chapter when we cover tips on using indices.

Record Keeping

Another important aspect of any genealogical research project is record keeping. There are many ways to maintain your records and entire books have been written about it. I want to make two points here that will be important to your success.

First, don't forget to record your unsuccessful research experiences. Most of us are very good about recording the details of what we find and where we found it, but we sometimes neglect to record what we did *not* find. For example, you review a particular microfilm looking for the birth record of your great-grandfather Pietro, but he is not on that film. So then you review the film containing the previous year's birth records. Well, he isn't on that one either, so next you review the film containing the following year's birth records, but to no avail.

Meanwhile, you never record the fact that you have searched for Pietro on these three microfilms. Several months later you decide to pursue his birth record again. Unless you have an extremely good memory, you will probably end up searching those same three microfilms again. This is a big waste of your time. You can see how simply recording your unsuccessful research now will save you a lot of time and frustration later.

If you use the methods outlined in this book, you really shouldn't be experiencing many research failures. In fact, you will probably be overwhelmed with success. And with each success you will have more answers to the Four Ws and will be able to create more specific research goals. Sometimes a single success may lead to several new research goals. For example, when you find your third great-grandparents' marriage record you learn each of their ages and places of birth. Now you can answer the when and where of their births and establish two new research goals: Find each of their birth records.

These new research goals need to be managed, especially if you only have time to pursue one goal at a time. I find that simply keeping a central list of future research goals is all it takes. This list acts as the map in your genealogical travels. It keeps you focused and moving forward in your research. It is also a great motivator! I just like to look at my list and smile because I know that almost every item on the list will lead to success! When you are ready to pursue a goal from your list, use the Italian

Genealogy Research Checklist form from Appendix D to guide you in your research.

Confirming Information

It is very important to always ensure that the record you have found is for the right person. This is especially critical in Italian records where many people share the same name. Fortunately, Italian vital records make this easy for us with frequent use of margin notations, referencing of women by their maiden names, and other tricks, which we will review in great detail in the section on actual records.

Also, don't believe everything you find in these records. People might have made mistakes when recording information and sometimes might have even lied. It is important to confirm everything that you find. Always try to seek out a second document that corroborates the information. If two documents give contradictory information, put more faith in the document that was recorded closer in time to the actual event and/or the document that was recorded by primary participants. For example, if the 1888 death record of your third great-grandfather, Giacomo, states that he was sixty years old at the time of his death (calculated birth year of 1828), but his marriage record of 1848 shows that he was twenty-five years old at marriage (calculated birth year of 1823), you may assume that the marriage record is the more accurate of the two. The marriage was recorded much closer to his birth than the death record. Also, the age at death was provided by a witness who might have estimated it, while Giacomo himself provided this information for the marriage document.

Most of all, don't make any blind assumptions. Don't assume that both the bride and groom were born in the same town where the marriage occurred. Don't assume all children in a family must be born in the same town. Any assumptions that you use in your research should be based on some evidence.

For More Information

These few points about general genealogical research guidelines are only the basics. For more detailed coverage on this topic I recommend the following books.

- *Applied Genealogy*, by Eugene Aubrey Stratton (Salt Lake City: Ancestry, Inc., 1988).
- *Genealogy as Pastime and Profession*, by Donald L. Jacobus (Baltimore: Genealogical Publishing Co. Inc., 1991).
- *Managing a Genealogical Project*, by William Dollarhide (Baltimore: Genealogical Publishing Co. Inc., 1993).
- *Unpuzzling Your Past*, by Emily Croom (Cincinnati: Betterway Books, 1995).

CHAPTER FOUR

History of Italy for the Genealogist

Italy's lively and interesting history shaped the lives of our ancestors. In order to understand our ancestors' culture, politics and motivations, we must understand the time periods in which they lived. Knowledge of the many political changes that occurred in Italy will also help us in our genealogical research because the maintenance of vital records varied greatly from one historical period to another.

Italy as we know it today has existed for only a little over 125 years. As a country, it is actually younger than the United States. Let's look briefly at the last few hundred years of Italy's history.

Before 1796

Up until the nineteenth century, the peninsula we now call Italy was made up of many autonomous city-states. These independent nations existed under successions of various invading empires of the French, Turks, Germans, Austrians and Spanish. The individual states, although sharing a small geographical space, were each culturally unique. They spoke separate dialects, worshiped in different churches and had unique attitudes.

There was no standardized record keeping at this time. However, the Council of Trent, in a decree confirmed by Pope Pius IV in 1564, required all Catholic priests to maintain written documentation for each of the major sacraments (baptism, marriage and extreme unction). These church records all contain essential information for genealogists, but they vary greatly in form, content and even language (some were written in Latin, some in Italian or a dialect, and some a combination). The only public records maintained at this time were recorded for the purpose of collecting taxes. Therefore, these records usually mention only people of some means.

Beginning in the late sixteenth century, there was an explosion of culture in Italy. The activities of artists, scholars, writers, musicians and scientists made this peninsula the cultural mecca of Europe. The baroque architecture of Bernini and his contemporaries flourished. The Italian opera began its popular history. The scientist Galileo made his greatest discoveries. The paintings and sculptures of this period are still viewed as masterpieces.

The cultural movement of the sixteenth and seventeenth centuries created a sense of nationalism within the future Italy for the first time. It encouraged the formation of an official written and spoken language. The increasing power of the church, established by the Council of Trent, also created a unifying force. Literacy was on the increase due to required scripture reading. This time period presented the first glimmer of the possibility of a unified Italy.

1796 - 1815

During this period, Napoleon, then the Emperor of France, began extending his control over much of Europe through a string of successful military victories. He began his invasion of Italy in 1796 and eventually liberated the autonomous city-states from their various foreign rulers. He politically unified them into the Kingdom of Italy, over which he proclaimed himself king. Only Sicily and Sardinia were not under Napoleon's control. An interesting note: Napoleon was born Napoleone Buonaparte in Italian-speaking Corsica and later changed his name to the French Bonaparte, so he was actually Italian, not French.

During his rule he created Italy's first centralized administrative, judicial and civil code. The feudalism that characterized the prior centuries was virtually eliminated.

His unification was not merely political, but social as well. The creation of new roads brought the previously isolated regions closer. This prompted commerce between regions, allowing a middle class to emerge. For the first time, the people could call themselves "Italian" and were not restricted to identifying themselves solely by their region.

The restructuring of Italy into organized regions, provinces and *comuni* (towns), with certain political responsibilities at the local level, was a Napoleonic creation. A similar form is still used today. Napoleon also initiated the maintenance of vital records for births, marriages and deaths throughout the kingdom. He not only detailed which records were to be kept and what information they must include, but also had special books printed to assist the town *sìndaco* (mayor) in maintaining this information.

By 1808, Napoleon controlled virtually all of continental Europe, either directly or through French rule. Only England, protected by the English Channel, kept him from becoming the sovereign of all Europe. Because he couldn't dominate England militarily, he tried to hurt the British economically by imposing a massive embargo on all British goods. The subjects of his empire, who were the consumers of these goods, began to stand up to Napoleon. With the help of British troops, they succeeded in overthrowing the French rule. First Spain, then Austria and Russia rebelled. Napoleon's troops failed miserably in Russia due to bad weather and poor preparations. This defeat encouraged other empires to reclaim their own territories. In 1815, at the Battle of Waterloo, Napoleon met his final defeat.

Although Napoleon's reign was short, its effects were far-reaching, particularly for those of us pursuing our Italian heritage. We have Napoleon to thank for the existence and consistency of Italy's vital records.

1815 - 1860

After Napoleon's fall, Italy reverted to its preunification autonomous city-states, and the European monarchs redrew their old boundaries. At this time, the northern states were ruled by the Austrian empire, the central region consisted of the papal states and Spain ruled the south.

It was impossible, however, for the Italians to return to their preunification social state. The suppression of human liberties, commonplace before Napoleon, was no longer tolerated. Secret underground societies, such as the *Carbonari*, developed to encourage a "free Italy." In the mid-1800s a movement called *il Risorgimento* (the resurrection) inspired a new Italy.

During this tumultuous period, many of the regions continued to maintain vital records as they had during the Napoleonic era, although they were no longer required to do so. Particularly in the south, you will often find no interruption in the records.

1860 - 1870

During this politically active decade, *il Risorgimento* and its encouragement of nationalism incited Victor Emmanual II (son of King Charles Albert of Sardinia, House of Savoy) and his prime minister, Cavour, to unite the individual kingdoms into a single empire. By 1870, Italy as we know it was born.

The newly unified Italy adopted a political structure almost identical to that of the original Napoleonic kingdom of Italy. Maintaining vital records was required again, using Napoleon's system—additional evidence that although Napoleon's reign was short, its influence was great.

This last major unification of Italy is important to genealogists because it played a major role in a sweeping emigration from Italy. It is ironic that the unification, with its intention to create a single land of prosperity, was indirectly responsible for this massive emigration. The causes of this exodus, as described briefly below, are reminiscent of a Rube Goldberg apparatus.

The last remnants of feudalism in the south were finally eliminated and the lands were divided among the common people. Since much of this land contained huge forests, the new small landowners had to clear the trees before they could farm. Within a decade, massive deforestation had occurred in southern Italy.

The topsoil, which was poor to begin with, now washed away during the rainy seasons, leaving the earth barren and unproductive. Raising crops was difficult in this environment.

The deforestation caused stagnant water to pool in the rainy months, increasing the mosquito population. Malaria epidemics were very common during this time period. Hundreds of thousands of people died and many others were left too ill to work and support themselves.

The promise of *il Risorgimento* to improve the socioeconomic status of the peasants was not realized. The benefits of the unification went primarily to the north, while the south was left frustrated and angry.

These conditions prompted the southern Italians to seek a better life in the Americas. At this time they had little to lose.

The Tie Between History and Genealogy

This brief history of Italy is important to our genealogical research because it helps explain why vital records were maintained (or not maintained) differently during these various time periods. The civil vital records for most regions begin in 1809, during the Napoleonic era. In most of the south, the maintenance of records continued after Napoleon's fall. Some areas may have gaps between the Napoleonic era and the 1865 reunification. All regions have records from 1865 to today.

The names of some provinces and towns changed during the last unification. For example, the province of Foggia in the region of Bari was called Capitanata before the unification. Some northern towns, such as the Austrian-named Bozen, took on Italian names (Bolzano). Although your ancestors may not have relocated, you may find the records under a different town or province during this time period. Table 4-1 compares the pre- and post-unification province names.

Geographical Organization of Italy

Italy's land is divided into regions, provinces and towns. Knowing the names of the regions, provinces and towns in which your ancestors lived is the key to one of the many doors you will have to unlock in your genealogical search.

Regions

Italy is divided into twenty *regióni* (regions), just like the U.S. is divided into fifty states. Examples of these Italian regions include Tuscany, Calabria, and Apulia. If you are familiar with Italian cooking you probably will recognize the names of some regions, because Italian cooking styles are regionally distinctive. The map in Figure 4-2 shows these twenty regions of Italy.

There is currently a proposal under consideration in Italy to reduce the number of regions to twelve. Will this affect your genealogical research? Probably not. The old vital records in which you are interested were all created at the local level. It is more important to know the name of the region at the time of the record's creation than the region's name today.

Provinces

Each region of Italy is divided into *provìnce* (provinces), just like the states of the U.S. are divided into counties. Some examples of provinces include Livorno (in the region of Tuscany), Cosenza (in the region of Calabria), and Bari (in the region of Apulia). There are a total of 103 provinces today, with a region containing from one to nine provinces. Recently, new provinces were created to accommodate the growing population in some areas. Figure 4-3 lists each region and its provinces while Figure 4-4 shows the locations of the provinces.

Towns

Each province is made up of *comuni* (cities or towns) and *frazióni* (villages or hamlets). For example, Elba is a city in the province of Livorno; Grimaldi is a city in the province of Cosenza, and Bari is a city in the province of Bari. Notice that Bari is both a city and a province. Each province has a capital city that shares its name. The map in Figure 4-2 shows the locations of the provincial capitals. When citing an Italian town, specify the town, province and region, as in Elba, Livorno, Tuscany.

In order to research Italian records, you need to know not only the region and province of your ancestor, but also the actual city or town, because the vital records were maintained at the town level. If

Region	Modern Provinces	Pre-Unification Names
Abruzzo	Chieti	Abruzzo Citra
	L'Aquila	Abruzzo Ultra
	Pescara	Abruzzo Ultra 1
	Teramo	Abruzzo Ultra 1
Basilicata	Matera	Basilicata
	Potenza	Basilicata
Calabria	Catanzaro	Calabria I'Ltra 2
	Cosenza	Calabria Citra
	Reggio Calabria	Calabria I'Ltra 1
Campania	Avellino	Principato I'Ltra
	Benevento	Principato I'Ltra
	Caserta	Molise, Principato I'Ltra, Terra Di
	Napoli	Lavoro
	Salerno	Napoli, Terra Di Lavoro
		Principato Citra
Emilia-Romagna	Bologna	Bologna
	Ferrara	Ferrara
	Forli	Forli
	Modena	Modena, Bologna
	Parma	Parma, Modena
	Piacenza	Parma
	Ravenna	Ravenna
	Regio Emilia	Modena
Fruili-Venezia Guilia	Gorizia	Austria
	Pordenone	Belluno, Udine
	Trieste	Austria
	Udine	Udine
Lazio	Frosinone	Frosinone
	Latina	Velletri, Frosinone
	Rieti	Rieti
	Roma	Roma
	Viterbo	Civita Vecchia, Viterbo
Liguria	Genova	Genova
	Imperia	Savona
	La Spezia	Genova
	Savona	Savona
Lombardia	Bergamo	Bergamo
	Brescia	Brescia
	Como	Como
	Cremona	Cremona
	Mantova	Mantua
	Milano	Milano, Lodi, Pavia
	Pavia	Allessandria, Novara, Vercelli
	Sondrio	Sondrio
	Varese	Como, Milano
Marche	Ancona	Ancona, Urbino
	Ascoli Piceno	Macerata
	Macerata	Ancona, Macerata
	Pesaro-Urbino	Urbino

FIGURE 4-1 **Modern Italian province names, by region, with their preunification (1870) names.**

Region	Modern Provinces	Pre-Unification Names
Molise	Campobasso	Capitanata, Molise
	Isernia	Molise
Piemonte	Alessandria	Alessandria
	Asti	Coni
	Cuneo	Coni
	Novara	Novara
	Torino	Torino
	Vercelli	Vercelli
Puglia	Bari	Terra di Bari
	Brindisi	Terra d'Otranto
	Foggia	Capitanata
	Lecce	Terra d'Otanto
	Taranto	Terra d'Otanto
Sardegna	Cagliari	Cagliari
	Nuoro	Nuoro
	Oristano	Nuoro
	Sassari	Sassari
Sicilia	Agrigento	Caltanisetta, Girgenti
	Caltanissetta	Caltanissetta
	Catania	Catania
	Enna	Catania
	Messina	Messina
	Palermo	Palermo
	Ragusa	Siragosa
	Siracusa	Siragosa
	Trapani	Trapani
Toscana	Arezzo	Arezzo
	Firenze	Firenze
	Grosseto	Grosseto
	Livorno	Pisa, Grosseto
	Lucca	Lucca
	Massa Carrara	Modena
	Pisa	Pisa
	Pistoia	Firenze
	Siena	Siena
Trentino-Alto Adige	Bolzano	Austria
	Trento	Austria
Umbria	Perugia	Perugia
	Terni	Perugia, Orvieto
Valle D'Aosta	Aosta	Aosta
Veneto	Belluno	Belluno, Treviso
	Padova	Padova
	Rovigo	Polesina
	Treviso	Treviso
	Venezia	Venezia
	Verona	Verona, Vicenza
	Vicenza	Vicenza

FIGURE 4-2 **Map of modern Italy showing regions and provincial capital cities.**

Modern Regions and Provinces of Italy

Abruzzo
1. Chieti
2. L'Aquila
3. Pescara
4. Teramo

Basilicata
5. Matera
6. Potenza

Calabria
7. Catanzaro
8. Cosenza
9. Crotone*
10. Reggio Calabria
11. Vibo Valentia*

Campania
12. Avellino
13. Benevento
14. Caserta
15. Napoli
16. Salerno

Emila-Romagna
17. Bologna
18. Ferrara
19. Forli
20. Modena
21. Parma
22. Piacenza
23. Ravenna
24. Regio Emilia
25. Rimini

Fruili-Venezia Guilia
26. Gorizia
27. Pordenone
28. Trieste
29. Udine

Lazio
30. Frosinone
31. Latina
32. Rieti
33. Roma
34. Viterbo

Liguria
35. Genova
36. Imperia
37. La Spezia
38. Savona

Lombardia
39. Bergamo
40. Brescia
41. Como
42. Cremona
43. Lecco*
44. Lodi*
45. Mantova
46. Milano
47. Pavia
48. Sondrio
49. Varese

Marche
50. Ancona
51. Ascoli Piceno
52. Macerata
53. Pesaro

Molise
54. Campobasso
55. Isernia

Piedmonte
56. Allessandria
57. Asti
58. Biella*
59. Cuneo
60. Novara
61. Torino
62. Verbano-Cusio-Ossola*
63. Vercelli

Puglia
64. Bari
65. Brindisi
66. Foggia
67. Lecce
68. Taranto

Sardegna
69. Cagliari
70. Nuoro
71. Oristano
72. Sassari

Sicilia
73. Agrigento
74. Caltanissetta
75. Catania
76. Enna
77. Messina
78. Palermo
79. Ragusa
80. Siracusa
81. Trapani

Toscana
82. Arezzo
83. Firenze
84. Grosseto
85. Livorno
86. Lucca
87. Massa-Carrara
88. Pisa
89. Pistoia
90. Prato*
91. Siena

Trentino-Alto Adige
92. Bolzano
93. Trento

Umbria
94. Perugia
95. Terni

Valle D'Aosta
96. Aosta

Veneto
97. Belluno
98. Padova
99. Rovigo
100. Treviso
101. Venezia
102. Verona
103. Vicenza

* added in 1993

FIGURE 4-3 **List of modern provinces by region (see facing map for locations).**

FIGURE 4-4 **Map of Italy showing the locations of the modern provinces (see facing list for province names).**

you have not yet determined the hometown of your immigrant ancestor, the next chapter will assist you with this.

Italian Naming Traditions and Their Ramifications

There has been a strong custom in Italy that determines how children are named:

- The first male is named after his paternal grandfather.
- The second male is named after his maternal grandfather.
- The first female is named after her paternal grandmother.
- The second female is named after her maternal grandmother.

The subsequent children could be named after the parents, a favorite aunt or uncle, a saint or a deceased relative. You will see evidence of this tradition throughout your family tree. Although this custom is pervasive, you should *never* use this as a method for assuming an ancestor's name. For example, if you know that your grandfather, Francesco, was the oldest son, don't automatically assume that his paternal grandfather was named Francesco. There are exceptions to this naming custom that preclude this assumption. Let's look at a few possible exceptions.

If your ancestor had a falling-out with his family and was estranged from them, he would probably not name his children after his parents. Or perhaps he was orphaned and didn't know his parents' names.

A more common exception to the naming tradition is seen in the following scenario. Giovanni Sorrentino names his firstborn son Luiggi, after his father. He has several other children that he names according to custom. When little Luiggi is about eight years old, he suddenly dies. This was not uncommon. Children often did not live to adulthood in pre-twentieth-century Italy. Since he now has no child named for his father, Giovanni will give the name Luiggi to his next son, who happens to be the fourth son. If you were to view the family at this time, the child who appears to be the oldest son is named after his maternal grandfather, not his paternal grandfather. The child named after his paternal grandfather is actually the fourth son. If you were to assume the names of the grandfathers in this situation, you would be wrong.

A final example of exceptions to the naming custom can be seen in the nontraditional family of my great-great-grandparents, Pasquale and Rosa. They were great opera fans who named all of their children after characters from their favorite operas. Due to these types of exceptions, you cannot use the Italian naming tradition to assume an ancestor's name.

This naming tradition has an even more important ramification in genealogical research. Because of the pervasiveness of this custom, you will find many people sharing the same name. Let's look at the following example.

Vito Savino marries a woman named Rosa and they have three sons, Pasquale, Domenico and Pietro, as shown in the following chart. Each of these sons marries and has his own children. According to custom, they will all name their first son Vito, after their father, and they will all name their first daughter Rosa, after their mother.

We have three Vito Savinos all born in the same town, within the same generation, possibly even born in the same year. The same situation exists for Rosa Savino. And *this* is a greatly simplified example since most Italians in this time period had more than three children! All the children would follow this naming tradition, even the daughters, although the daughters would name the second son and second daughter after the maternal grandparents.

Now, you come along looking for the birth record of your great-great-grandfather, Vito Savino. You have answered all four *W*s of your research goal, so you know where and when he was born, but you do not know his parents' names. You find these three Vito Savinos, but how do you know which one is your great-great-grandfather?

An even worse situation could occur if you first find Vito Savino number two (son of Domenico) and stop searching because you assume that you have found your great-great-grandfather. Meanwhile, Vito Savino number three (son of Pietro) is really your ancestor. You now begin pursuing the ancestors of Vito Savino number two. On the pater-

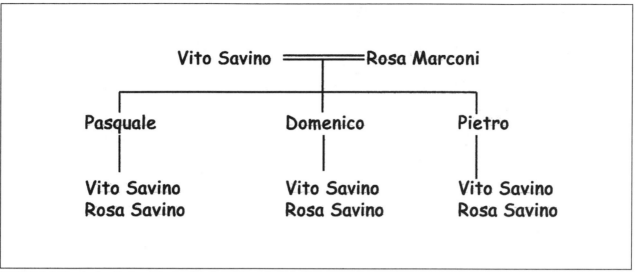

FIGURE 4-5 **Simple family tree illustrating how the common Italian naming tradition results in many people sharing the same name.**

nal side you will at least be on the right track, but on his maternal side you will be barking up the wrong family tree and not even know it.

At first blush, this logic creates a frightening situation. How can you ever know if you've found the right ancestor?

Well, don't panic. There are methods you can use to insure that you're working on the right ancestor. We briefly reviewed some of these methods in a general fashion in the last chapter. Later, we will get more detailed and talk about margin notations and the appropriate sequence in which to pursue records.

The important point to retain from this discussion is that due to the Italian naming tradition, you will find many people with the same names. Therefore, you must be absolutely certain to confirm that you have found your direct ancestor.

Nineteenth-Century Italian Society

Italy in the nineteenth century was a society divided by class. The aristocrats, the smallest class, consisted of great land barons and titled families. They lived primarily in the large cities and rarely visited their landholdings.

An emerging middle class consisted mainly of the educated (lawyers, notaries, etc.) and merchants. These individuals usually were referred to by a title

of respect, such as *dòn* (sir), *signóre* (mister) or *maèstro* (master).

The largest class, the *contadini* (peasants), consisted of laborers and farmers. Most of us are descendants from this group. There was very little interaction between these classes. A member of one class could never even consider aspiring to improve his or her position and move up to a higher class.

Although education was made available to everyone, the poor could not afford to send their children to school since they were needed to work and provide income to help support the family. At five or six years old, many children were already working.

Although some *contadini* were small landowners, they were still poor and would always be poor. Their plot of land was usually only large enough to support one family, so only the first son could inherit the land. Since the family was poor, they could only afford a small dowry for the first daughter. Because of this situation, frequently only the first male and the first female of these families could afford to marry. The other children often remained unmarried, resulting in many unwanted pregnancies and abandoned foundlings.

Even among the poor, marriages were often arranged. When their children were still babies, a couple might promise a daughter to the son of a friend or neighbor. In any case, the parents had to approve of their children's marriages, and love was often less important than convenience. During the emigrations from Italy to North and South America, daughters were frequently shipped off to a foreign land to marry the friend of a cousin or another complete stranger who had established himself in the new land.

The typical house of a common family was a small (sometimes only one room) stone, brick or mud construction, usually one story. Of course, there was no running water or drainage. This tiny abode often housed large extended families, and sometimes chickens, goats or other animals. Because of this crowding and lack of privacy, the streets and piazzas of the town were the living rooms of the community. Almost all socializing, celebrating and recreation occurred in public.

Family was a major focus in the lives of the *contadini*. Although the family structure appears to be patriarchal to the outsider, there is a hidden, but strong, matriarchal influence. The father's public role was to act as the ultimate authority over all family matters, but his will was usually a reflection of the mother's wishes. In public, the women usually held a subservient role, catering to the men and taking care of the home and family, as well as working outside the home.

Religion also played a major role in the life of the *contadini*. They were not religious in the modern sense, but prayed and went to church out of fear, superstition and obligation. They were enthralled by the pageantry of religious ceremonies and fascinated by the stories of the Bible and the lives of the saints. All events were attributed to the will of God or a saint, so praying was a way of possibly swaying events. Each town had a patron saint, whose feast day was celebrated annually with feasts, parades and parties, with the hope that the saint would protect the town throughout the coming year.

A Typical Day in the Life of a Nineteenth-Century Peasant

Since it provided the light needed to work, the sun was the alarm clock. Workdays were shorter in the winter and longer in the summer. Rising from a wooden plank bed, covered with a mattress stuffed with crunchy dried cornstalks, the typical peasant would get dressed and put on wooden shoes (only the wealthy wore leather shoes).

First the animals (if there were any) had to be tended. Chicken eggs were collected to be sold. They were never eaten by the peasants because they were too valuable. All animal droppings (and human, as well) were collected and stored in a wooden bin, awaiting the daily arrival of the man with the wooden cart who would purchase this fertilizer to use in the fields.

The water for drinking, cooking and washing had to be carried from the village's central well or fountain. These fountains became the meeting place for the exchange of news and gossip. In some rocky regions, a water vendor, hauling urns of water up the steep hills with a mule-drawn wooden cart, sold this precious commodity from door to door.

Breakfast usually consisted of a chunk of bread or maybe a bowl of polenta (cornmeal mush) in the north. Frequently breakfast was not eaten upon arising but at a mid-morning break from work.

The men who were not fortunate enough to hold regular jobs would work as day laborers. Bosses would come to the town square with a wagon looking for men to spend a day or so hauling stone, picking rice or grapes, or clearing land. The day laborers never knew if they would be working from one day to the next.

The women would work in the fields or in a nearby factory. The silk industry was very big and, without modern technology, required many hands to wind, spin and weave the silk threads. The women's hands were rough, raw and pained from the exposure to boiling hot water and the constant twisting of the threads.

Even the children worked, from as young as five years old. They would help pick rice or grapes at harvest time. The little girls would begin their silk factory "careers" by manually turning the wheels for the silk spinners.

At lunchtime, most peasants would consume a boiled potato, a chunk of bread or a weak soup made from onions and water, and then go back to work.

As the sun began to set and it became too dark

to see, the work day was over. The evening meal would be just a little more substantial than the day's other repasts. Cabbage soup, a boiled potato, pasta (in the south), or polenta (in the north) would be the main course, rounded out with some bread. Meat was rarely eaten by peasants except on Sundays or feast days (holidays), and even then their rice or pasta soup would have a weak meat broth with a few shreds of meat floating in it. Wine would also be consumed on these special days.

The evening finally allowed time for socializing. People walked through the streets, gathered and talked. Children ran around and played. In the winter, when it was too cold and dark to spend the evening in the streets, people would gather in a barn, warmed only by the bodies of the animals and lit by a single oil lamp. Wood and coal were too valuable to be burned just for warmth and were reserved solely for cooking. In the barn, the women would knit or spin while they talked in one corner. The men, in a different corner, would tell stories or play gambling games.

When it was time to retire, the peasants would return to their homes and go to bed, often with the whole family sharing sleeping quarters. The next morning, the peasant's day was repeated. The peasants had no goals or long-term accomplishments to meet. They lived a day-to-day existence, punctuated by church on Sundays, when they had the day off from work, and the anticipation of the next feast day.

CHAPTER FIVE

Determining Your Immigrant Ancestor's Hometown

In order to find and use the Italian vital records of your ancestors, you must know the name of the town where the events occurred, because that is where the documents were created. The link between that Italian town and your family heritage is your original immigrant ancestor. That ancestor, born in Italy and migrating to a new life in North America, is the key to unlocking the treasures to be found in the Italian *Stato Civile*.

This chapter will show you how to discover the Italian town of your ancestors. If you already have this information from family stories, you should still read this chapter and check the resources described here to confirm that you do, in fact, have the correct town. I was told by my grandmother that my grandfather's father was from Caserta. Caserta is not only a city, but a province as well. I couldn't be sure if he was from the actual city of Caserta, or a small town in the province of Caserta, until I checked all resources.

There are three sections to this chapter. The first covers the Italian immigration to North America. The information and statistics provided here, aside from being interesting, will help you narrow down your search. The section on American resources discusses the primary sources of information available, such as census records and ship passenger lists, as well as some secondary sources. Finally, we will cover some Italian resources.

Italian Immigration to North America

Italians have been coming to North America since the original discoverer, Cristoforo Colombo, in 1492. But only mere handfuls of Italians had migrated by 1820. From about that time through the mid-1800s, the immigration numbers increased as a few dozen to several hundred Italians arrived in the Americas each year. These immigrants were pre-dominately from northern Italy and were members of the upper-middle class. They consisted of skilled artisans, merchants, intellectuals, aristocrats and political exiles, and they settled primarily in the major cities of New York, Boston and Philadelphia.

The next wave of Italian immigration began in the 1850s, when more than one thousand Italians arrived each year. These migrants were poor Italians who came here mainly for economic reasons. This group created the original Italian settlements in New Orleans and San Francisco.

The next tide of Italian immigration was massive. From 1876 until 1930, more than 4.5 million Italians entered the United States, representing 89 percent of the total Italian immigration from 1820 through 1970. No other ethnic group in history sent so many people to the U.S. in so short a period of time. The driving force behind this was economic, as discussed in chapter four. As the graph in Figure 5-1 shows, peak immigration occurred between 1902 and 1921. The major drop during World War I was due to Italy's suspended emigration of military-aged men.

Since 89 percent of the Italian immigration to the United States occurred between 1876 and 1930, most of us are descended from the immigrants of this time period. Thus, we are only second- or third-generation Americans. This fact means that it should not be too difficult to learn the hometown of your original immigrant ancestor. You may have living relatives that know this information. Also, record keeping was well established by this time and the many documents kept during this period will assist you in finding the answer.

Between 1876 and 1930, most Italian immigrants (80 percent) came from southern Italy, as shown in Figure 5-2. This statistic could be helpful if your family tradition states that your immigrant ancestor came from a town, such as Altavilla, that does not have a unique name. There are three Altavillas; one in the north and two in the south. If you have no other clues to help you determine which one is the birthplace of your ancestor, simple probability will tell you to check the southern towns first.

Figure 5-2 also shows the breakdown of the southern immigrants by Italian region. The largest numbers came from Sicily and Campania. Again, this data can assist you with duplicated town names. For example, your family tradition says that Lecce is the place of your Italian heritage, but there are two Lecces, both in the south, one in Abruzzi and one in Apulia. If you have no other evidence to determine which one is the Lecce you are looking for, try searching the Lecce in Abruzzi first, since it is more likely than the Lecce in Apulia to be the correct one.

North American Resources

To determine the hometown of your immigrant ancestor, you will use primarily North American re-

sources. Although the focus of this book is on Italian resources, specifically Italian vital records, we will take a short detour here to discuss some American records that are critical in discovering your Italian ancestral town. This section is useful not only for Italian ancestors, but applies to immigrants from any country.

A general genealogical rule states that one must go from the known to the unknown. In our discussion here, the Italian hometown is the unknown. The act of immigration to the United States is the known. You cannot jump directly to the unknown without first exhausting all the elements of the known, the North American resources. The resources covered here are the known documents that will lead you back to the unknown Italian town.

Name Changes

In order to research the North American resources covered in this chapter, you need to know your immigrant ancestor's full name. In order to research the Italian records covered in the rest of this book,

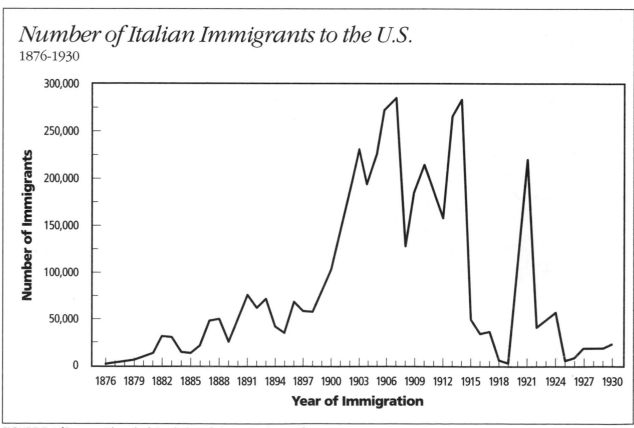

FIGURE 5-1 (Source: Historical Statistics of the United States)

you must know the full name that your ancestor carried in Italy. The surname your Italian family carries today may not be the same name that your immigrant ancestor used back in Italy. It may have been changed at any point between the time of emmigration from Italy and today. If the surname has changed, the change probably occurred during the time covered by the North American records. The major reasons for surname changes include illiteracy, Americanization, simplification and evasion of authorities.

The most common cause of name changes of immigrants was illiteracy. The majority of immigrants arriving in the United States were illiterate, and when the immigration officials were recording their information, the immigrant was generally unable to spell his or her own name. Thus, the officials wrote it as it sounded. Because Italian is written basically like it sounds to English-speaking ears (with a few exceptions discussed below), the Italian names were butchered less often than other ethnic groups, such as the Polish. In most cases, extra letters were dropped, such as the name Nanno becoming Nano. These variations are easy to determine.

The more difficult variations occur with the letters *c* and *g*. In Italian, the letters *ch* are pronounced like a *k* sound, possibly resulting in the Italian name Chieti turning into an English version, Ketti. Also, the letters *ci* are pronounced like the sound *ch*, possibly resulting in the Italian name Ciuccio turning into the written Chucho. The letters *gi* in Italian are pronounced as a *j* sound. Thus the Italian name of Giuliano may have become Juliano.

Italian/English dictionaries usually contain a pronunciation table in the front. Use this to determine all possible variations of your Italian surnames, and keep them in mind while researching the American documents.

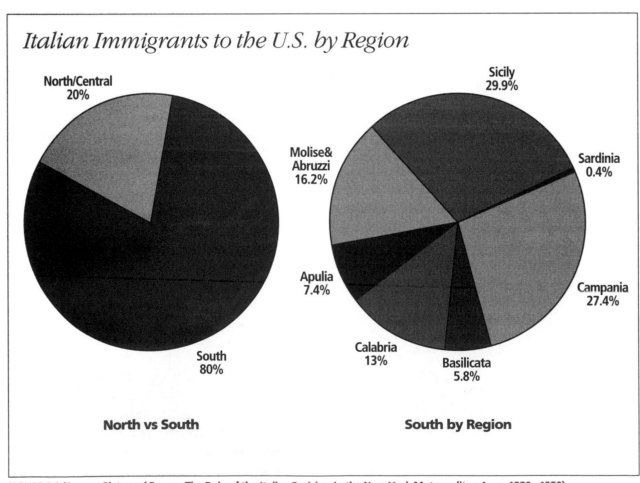

FIGURE 5-2 (Source: Piety and Power: The Role of the Italian Parishes in the New York Metropolitan Area, 1880 - 1930)

Another cause of name changes of Italian immigrants is Americanization. Some Italian names were simply translated from Italian to English, either by immigration officials or, later when the immigrants became naturalized citizens, by the judge. Examples of this include the Italian name Duca becoming Duke, or Bianco becoming the English, White. Some immigrants purposefully Americanized their surname in order to avoid the then rampant discrimination against Italians. For example, by dropping the *i* in the Italian name Bartoni, the name becomes Barton, a more American-sounding name.

Simplification was another reason for name changes. Names that were long, hard to spell, or difficult to pronounce often became shortened for convenience. The surname Pasqualicchio, for example, could be simplified to Pasqua.

Finally, some immigrants changed their names completely in order to avoid the authorities. Italian men could not emigrate if they had not served their mandatory military service, nor could men of military age emigrate at all during World War I. Consequently, those men that did leave Italy under these conditions changed their names so they could not be tracked down by the authorities. Trying to determine an immigrant's real name in this situation is very difficult.

Try to determine all possible variations of your Italian surname and keep them in mind when researching the North American documents. For example, if you cannot find your immigrant ancestor under his known surname in the 1920 census, try using one of the variations of the name. As you go back in time through the North American records you might find when and how your ancestor's name changed. And if it has changed, now you know the surname used in Italy so you can next pursue the Italian records.

The Basic Facts Required

In order to discover your immigrant ancestor's hometown you must have three basic pieces of information: his or her full name, an approximate year of birth, and an approximate year of immigration. If you have more information, such as names of parents or siblings, or the name of the arrival ship, that is even better.

These three pieces of information may be found in the various American resources discussed below. Each resource may add one or two more pieces of information to the puzzle and eventually lead you to the answer.

Primary Versus Secondary Sources

It is very important to understand the difference between primary and secondary sources of information. A primary source of information is a record that was created contemporaneously with the event that it describes. For example, a birth certificate showing an individual's mother and father is considered a primary source for proving a descendence. A secondary source is one that was created after the event. For example, a published genealogy may also show a descendence, but is considered a secondary source since it is merely a collection of information gathered and presented by its author.

Primary sources of information are obviously better than secondary sources. Your research should always focus on primary sources and only resort to secondary sources when all primary sources have been exhausted. Secondary sources can be used to find primary sources. For example, you do not know when or where your immigrant ancestor died. However, your cousin heard a great-aunt once say that he died in 1941 in Chicago. This is a secondary source of information. Instead of simply taking it as a fact, use it to find the primary source—the death certificate. Since you now have a clue as to the the place and year of death, you can seek out his death certificate. Without this clue, you may not have been able to obtain the death certificate at all.

When using a primary source in your research, always take the information with a grain of salt. When using secondary sources, try a pound of salt. Primary sources should be confirmed by additional primary sources. Secondary sources should be used to point you in the right direction of the primary sources.

There are four major primary North American resources for determining your immigrant ancestor's hometown, and several minor ones. The four major resources include census records, naturalization records, ship passenger lists and passport applications. The minor resources include family documents (letters, etc.), church records, cemetery records and newspapers.

Interviews With Family and Friends
The first place to start your research is with your own family. Talk to parents, grandparents, aunts, uncles, cousins and old family friends. You will be surprised at the information you can obtain. Of course, this information is considered a secondary source, so use it only to guide you in your research.

Don't just call them on the phone and ask questions; visit these important people. Ask them to show you any old documents, letters, memorial cards or photographs they may have. They may have forgotten they have your great-grandfather's Italian passport until it falls out from between a stack of old photos. Reviewing these old pieces of memorabilia will suddenly jog their memories, and great stories will begin to flow from them. Even if you don't obtain any clues to the name of your Italian ancestral hometown, you will have discovered personal stories about your ancestors that cannot be found anywhere else!

Primary Sources
Once you have interviewed relatives and family friends, it's time to begin searching primary sources.

Census Records
The federal census records should be the first primary sources you pursue. Since 1850, the federal census includes each resident's name and age. This age can be used to determine an approximate birth year. Since 1900, the year of immigration and naturalization information are also shown on the federal census records, providing other important clues. The resident's place of birth is also shown on the federal census records. However, it usually simply states the name of the country.

Federal censuses are taken only once every decade. The most recent federal census available to the public is the one taken in 1920. Census records less than seventy-four years old are not released to the public. To find a census record, you must know your ancestor's state of residence and his or her name. The 1900 and 1920 census records are indexed by Soundex code, a method that emphasizes sound over spelling. The 1910 census is only partially indexed.

Federal census records are available on microfilm from many sources. The National Archives in Washington, DC, and their twelve regional branches have all films available; you can call (202) 501-5130 to find the nearest branch. The Family History Library in Salt Lake City has all federal census films, while their branches throughout the country have the films for their local areas (although any film can be ordered at any local Family History Center). The Family History Library is discussed in chapter nine. Major public libraries and university libraries in major cities usually carry the census films for their state. If you cannot find a source of federal census records near you, contact a local genealogical society and ask them to point you to the nearest source.

State census records, although varying widely from state to state, may also provide you with important information. Because the 1890 federal census was almost completely destroyed by fire, there is no federal census between 1880 and 1900, a period when many Italian immigrants arrived here. The state census records fill this gap. Some state census records also include more information than their federal counterparts. For example, New York state census records include the date and place of naturalization, which will help locate the naturalization documents. State census records may be found in state archives, major libraries and the Family History Library.

Check all the census years that are available to confirm that the information is correct. Sometimes a child or neighbor answered the census-takers' questions and may have estimated the information. Once you have located your immigrant ancestor in a census record, you should now have his or her approximate year of birth and the year of immigration. You may also have learned if and when your ancestor became naturalized.

As a bonus, your discoveries will include your ancestor's exact address, occupation, literacy status and other personal pieces of information. You are now starting to build a mental image of your ancestor and his or her life.

Naturalization Documents

Naturalization is the process of becoming an American citizen. If your census research shows that your ancestor was naturalized, your next step will be to seek the naturalization documents. Even if you believe that your ancestor was not naturalized, you should check these sources anyway, because he or she might have completed only the first phase of the naturalization process.

Naturalization was a two-step process. First, the immigrant had to file a declaration of intention, often called "first papers," to become a citizen. Then, after a two- to seven-year period (depending on the prevailing regulations), the petition for naturalization could be filed and approved and the immigrant was granted citizenship. After 1941, a declaration of intention was no longer necessary.

Compared to other ethnic groups, Italian immigrants had one of the lowest percentages of naturalization. However, the percentage of Italians filing the declaration of intention was one of the highest. So even if your ancestor was not naturalized, you may still find the first papers.

Until 1922, wives and children of naturalized immigrants were automatically granted citizenship, so it is not necessary to search for separate naturalization documents for family members prior to this period.

The naturalization documents could be filed in any court (federal, state or county), so you may have to search several jurisdictions. After 1906, all courts had to send a copy of the documentation to the Bureau of Immigration in Washington, DC, so if your ancestor was naturalized after this year you can obtain this information from a single source.

The genealogical information contained in the naturalization documents varies greatly from one jurisdiction to another and from year to year. You may learn nothing new about your ancestor or you may hit the mother lode and discover birth date, birthplace, and the date and ship of immigration. Generally, naturalization documents processed after 1906 contain more valuable genealogical information.

You may obtain naturalization documents from several sources. For those processed after 1906, you can write to the Bureau of Immigration and Naturalization (425 I Street, Room 5304, Washington, DC 20536) and ask for an application. The National Archives has microfilms of the naturalization papers filed in federal courts as well as those of the New York District Courts. These New York records are particularly valuable for Italian research because the majority of Italian immigrants arrived at the port of New York. Many remained there. State archives will have the naturalization records filed in state courts. Of course, the Family History Library has access to all of these microfilmed documents.

One caveat is necessary for the naturalization documents. It is possible that the information they contain may be false. In their desire to quickly become American citizens, some immigrants purposefully misrepresented their arrival date to the United States. For example, my great-great-grandfather actually arrived in the United States in 1899. The federal census and his ship's passenger list confirm this. He filed his declaration of intention in 1900 and stated that he arrived in 1894, five years earlier than he really did, presumably because the naturalization law at that time required residency of more years than he wanted to wait. This is just another example of how important it is to find several sources that confirm all genealogical information. If I had first discovered the declaration of intention and didn't look for other sources to prove the immigration year, I could have spent much time looking unsuccessfully for his inclusion in a ship manifest from 1894.

Ships' Passenger Lists

Once you have learned the approximate year of birth of your immigrant ancestor and the approximate year of immigration, you can search for the passenger list of the ship on which he or she arrived. These lists are fascinating because you can learn not only important genealogical information, such as last residence and birthplace, but also more personal information, such as how much money your ancestor was carrying, a physical description and if he or she was traveling with family and friends.

To narrow down your search you should know your ancestor's port of arrival. There were five major ports of immigration (Baltimore, Boston, New Orleans, New York and Philadelphia) and many minor ones. If you are not certain which port your ancestor used, you may have to search the records for several ports. Since 97 percent of Italian immigrants arriving between 1880 and 1925 entered through New York, you may want to start with this port.

There were two major periods for the passenger lists, 1565 to 1819 and 1820 to 1954. The existing lists from 1565 to 1819 are not centralized, but many of them are published in books and periodicals. In 1819, Congress required captains to submit a passenger manifest at embarkation. The lists from 1820 to 1954 are centralized by the National Archives and are available on microfilm. We will focus on the lists from this period, since most Italian immigration occurred during this time. Keep in mind that not every ship's passenger list is available. Some were lost or destroyed.

The manifests from this period can be further divided into Customs Lists (1820 to 1891) and Immigration Lists (1891 to 1954). The former were the responsibility of the Bureau of Customs and include very basic information, such as name, age, sex, occupation and nationality. In 1891 the Bureau of Immigration was established and became responsible for all immigration affairs. The Immigration Lists contain a great deal of information and are very consistent because the federal government printed standard forms for recording the data. The information on these manifests includes name, age, sex, marital status, occupation, ability to read or write, nationality, last residence, final destination in the United States and whether they had a ticket to that destination, amount of money in their possession, if they had been to the United States before and other interesting and useful information.

Indices to Ships' Passenger Lists

If you know the actual ship on which your ancestor arrived and the year of arrival, or if you know the actual date and place of arrival, you can go directly to the ship manifest. If you are not fortunate enough to have this information, you must use an index to find your ancestor's ship. You certainly don't want to search through rolls of microfilm (the lists for New York arrivals between 1897 and 1957 take up almost 8,900 rolls of film!).

There are several types of indices available. The major indices to the ships' passenger lists have been microfilmed by the National Archives and were compiled during the 1930s as part of the Work Projects Administration. The WPA was a federal program that provided jobs for the unemployed. However, not all years for all ports were indexed during this project. For example, the New York lists between 1846 and 1897 were not indexed, a period and port that include many Italian immigrants.

If the National Archives indices don't cover your ancestor's port and year of arrival, you can use other published indices. There are thousands of published ships' passenger lists in books and periodicals. A good reference to many of these published sources is *Passenger and Immigration Lists Bibliography, 1538 - 1900* by P. William Filby. This publication lists over 2,500 published lists, indexed by port of arrival, port of embarkation, ethnic group and state. You can use this resource to find an index that may lead you to your ancestor.

A wonderful series of published passenger lists for Italian researchers is *Italians to America: Lists of Passengers Arriving at U.S. Ports, 1880-1899* edited by Ira A. Glazier and P. William Filby. This projected twelve-volume series (still in process) indexes Italian immigrant passenger list information. The first eight volumes focus on arrivals at the port of New York. This helps fill that critical gap in the WPA index for New York. The following volumes are currently available:

Volume 1—Passengers Arriving at New York Jan. 1880-Dec. 1884
Volume 2—Passengers Arriving at New York Jan. 1885-June 1887
Volume 3—Passengers Arriving at New York July 1887-June 1889

Volume 4—Passengers Arriving at New York July 1889-Oct. 1890

Volume 5—Passengers Arriving at New York Nov. 1890-Dec. 1891

Volume 6—Passengers Arriving at New York Jan. 1892-Dec. 1892

Volume 7—Passengers Arriving at New York Jan. 1893-Sept. 1893

There are more volumes planned for New York and additional volumes to cover other ports of entry. This series is a valuable resource to researchers of Italian immigrant ancestors.

If you are unable to find your ancestor in any of the indices, it doesn't necessarily mean that they are not on a passenger list. Maybe a bleary-eyed indexer accidentally missed your ancestor or made a mistake when recording the information. Try searching the indices for a family member or traveling companion. Italian immigrants generally traveled with family members, friends or neighbors. Family, friends and neighbors in Italy often settled in the same neighborhood in North America. Because censuses are taken according to geographical location, those listed above and below your ancestors were their neighbors. If they immigrated in the same year as your ancestor, it is possible they traveled together. Try finding the ships' passenger list for the neighbor, and you may find your ancestor on the same ship.

Also try searching indices for other ports of entry. Even though your ancestor actually arrived in Boston, it is possible that the ship first stopped in New York and that the passenger lists were processed there.

If there are no indices for your ancestor's year of immigration or you are unable to find him or her in the indices, you may have to search the actual lists. This task should be a last resort tactic because it can be a massive project. You may wish to try the remaining sources covered in this chapter first. In any case, you need to narrow down the possible ship lists as much as possible. Knowing just the year of immigration is not enough since there could be hundreds of ships arriving from Italy in a single year. Your ancestor may not have even departed from Italy. Knowing the name of the ship will narrow your search even more. For a list of ships arriving from various Italian ports by date, use the *Morton-Allen Directory of European Passenger Steamship Arrivals*, available at libraries and genealogical archives.

There are two important tips of which you should be aware when researching ships' passenger lists for your Italian ancestors. First, women traveling without their husbands usually traveled under their maiden names. You will find entries for a mother and her children with the children using their father's last name and the mother using her maiden name. Therefore, you must search for both names when reviewing the indices.

Second, you may find your immigrant ancestor on more than one list. Many Italians traveled back and forth between Italy and the United Stated several times, earning the nickname, "birds of passage." Frequently, a husband would arrive first, get settled, and then return to Italy to bring back his wife and children. Many Italian men also returned annually, working part of the year in the United States (earning a good salary) and spending the rest of the year in Italy with their family. These immigrants may be found on more than one ship passenger list. You might want to try searching the indices of years other than the initial immigration year to see if your ancestor was a "bird of passage." Even if you have found the list for the original immigration, subsequent lists could confirm what you know and even provide additional information, since the format of ships' passenger lists varied across the years.

Passport Applications

Passports, although not actually required for travel until 1941, may provide some important genealogical information. If your immigrant ancestor was a naturalized citizen and traveled back to Italy, he or she may have applied for a U.S. passport to expedite the reentry process.

Passport applications generally include naturalization information, birth date and birthplace of the immigrant and his or her family members, occupation and a physical description. Since 1914 they have also included a photograph.

Passport applications from 1791 to 1925 were microfilmed by the National Archives. These films are also available at the Family History Library. They are indexed primarily by date of departure or issue, and then roughly alphabetically. Remember to search for Italian women under both their maiden and married names. Check this resource for your immigrant ancestor, and you may discover a photograph!

Secondary American Resources

We have just covered four major primary American resources that may help you determine the Italian hometown of your immigrant ancestor. If you are unsuccessful with these resources, you may want to try some other primary resources such as church records, cemetery records, newspapers, city directories, etc. These resources are harder to find and may offer information that is of little genealogical value. Before attempting to research these miscellaneous primary resources, you may wish to try reviewing some secondary resources.

Secondary resources are those that contain genealogical information, but were created after the events, such as a published genealogy. Remember, the information obtained from these sources should be verified. When you're stuck, secondary resources may be just what you need to point you to the primary resources and get you started. We'll review two types of secondary resources: genealogical databases and published genealogies.

Genealogical Databases

Genealogical databases are simply indexed lists (usually stored on some form of electronic media) containing names, dates and places. These databases are compiled from information submitted by people who are researching their family trees for the purpose of sharing known information and finding others pursuing the same family lines. If you find an ancestor's name in any of these databases, remember, it is just a secondary source. Use any information you may find here to guide you in your research. Seek out primary sources to confirm it.

Two major genealogical databases, available at the Family History Library and its branches (discussed in chapter nine), are the International Genealogical Index (IGI) and the Ancestral File. Both of these databases are stored on CD-ROM and are accessed via a computer using powerful search techniques that allow you to quickly locate information by name, location and/or date ranges. Some major libraries also have these databases available.

The IGI consists of individual events—for example, John Smith's christening. A reference is included for each event, so you can obtain the primary source. The latest edition (1996) of the IGI contains over 200 million names. These names are from vital records from all over the world (early 1500s to 1885) and also include names submitted by members of The Church of Jesus Christ of Latter-day Saints (Mormons). The Family History Library is run by the Mormons and is explained in more detail in chapter nine.

The Ancestral File contains families and pedigrees. Once you find a person here, you can usually go through their pedigree and view the whole family. This information comes from people throughout the world wanting to share their family history with others. The name and address of the submitter is included (and possibly references for the data). If you have an unknown distant cousin who has already researched your family line, this may be the place to find him or her. If you don't find any of your family lines here, you may wish to contribute your own family history to this database for future researchers.

There are many other genealogical databases available on the Internet and commercial online services. A large one worth mentioning is GenServ. GenServ is an ever-growing database of files containing family lines. These files are submitted by people like you, interested in their family history and wanting to share the fruits of their research. For more information about using this database, connect to the Internet location:

http://soback.kornet.nm.kr/~cmanis/

A final database of particular interest to Italians is the one compiled by POINT. POINT (*P*ursuing *O*ur *I*talian *N*ames *T*ogether) is an organization of people interested in their Italian ancestry. Members submit the surnames, regions, provinces and towns of their Italian ancestors to POINT, and POINT publishes the data in the form of an annual directory. Members discover others pursuing the same names in the same locations and then communicate to share information. A surprising number of people discover distant cousins here. You may submit names to the database without becoming a member. As a member, however, you receive not only the annual directory, but a subscription to the quarterly journal as well. POINT's address is: P.O. Box 2977, Palo Verdes, CA 90274.

You may search all of the above mentioned databases and find no mention of your Italian ancestors, which is what happened to me. In any case, you may wish to submit your own family tree to these databases. Maybe some long lost cousin will scc it, contact you and provide you with some missing information.

Published Genealogies

Published books, such as genealogies, biographies and histories, are another form of secondary resources that may help you in your research. These are available in major libraries, the Family History Library and the Library of Congress.

There are thousands of compiled genealogies that have been published, and your ancestor may be mentioned in one of them. Search the library catalogs first using your ancestor's surname as the subject, then as the author.

Many collective biographies have been published, such as *Leading Americans of Italian Descent in Massachusetts*, containing biographical sketches of many individuals. There are also histories of Italian communities in America, such as *The Italians in Chicago: A Study of Americanization*, which also mention names of prominent Italian immigrants. To find these types of publications, search the library catalog using "Italian" and the name of a state or city for the subject.

Italian Resources

If you have exhausted all the North American documents and are still not sure of the Italian town, there are a few Italian resources that may help you. These

should be used only after you have thoroughly researched the American records.

There are three types of Italian resources that may assist in finding the name of your ancestor's birthplace: Italian gazetteers, military records and books of Italian surnames.

Italian Gazetteers

A gazetteer is a book of geographic locations, specifically cities, towns and hamlets. If you know the name of the town but not the region or province, a gazetteer will provide that missing information. It also gives population, postal codes, military districts, and other information.

Another use for a gazetteer is to help you find the correct name and spelling of a particular town. For example, my great-great-aunt told me the name of the birthplace of her mother (my great-great-grandmother). She said it in a rush of Italian syllables that sounded like "*Santa Maria Capovetta*." When I asked her how it was spelled, she didn't know. She had heard the name during her childhood and repeated it to me as she remembered it. I looked it up in an Italian gazetteer. It was *Santa Maria di Capua Vetere*. If I hadn't found the correct spelling in the gazetteer, I would have been searching in vain for the wrong town!

You can find Italian gazetteers in major libraries. The Family History Library offers one on microfilm. Its title is *Nuovo dizionario dei comuni e frazioni di comuni con le circonscrizioni amministrative* (New dictionary of towns and hamlets with their administrative districts). The film number is 0795276 and it may be ordered at any local Family History Center.

Military Records

All Italian records of genealogical value were created at the local town level with one exception, military records. Military records were maintained at the military district level. This means that if you only know the name of the province of your ancestor, you may be able to use the military records to determine his birthplace. If you are searching for a female ancestor, try using the military records to find her brother or father.

When Italy was unified the last time, a new law was enacted requiring all males to register with the military shortly before their twentieth birthday. This means that all males born since about 1850 should have a military record in the registers of the Office of Conscription (*registri degli Uffici di Leva*). Even if they didn't qualify for military service (due to health or family conditions) or emigrated before they were old enough to register, there will still be a document recording their military status.

These records were created by the military district. A province may have from one to six military districts, so if you don't know the town of your ancestor but know the province, you can narrow down your search to a couple of military districts. Use a gazetteer (mentioned above) to determine the military districts for a particular province.

The *registri di Leva* are organized into annual conscription classes (each class containing the young men who will turn twenty that year). If you know your ancestor's approximate year of birth, you can narrow down your search to only a few years of records. Each year is indexed by name, so it is easy to find a particular person.

Once you find your ancestor in these records, you will have learned his town of birth and can begin pursuing other vital records. You will also discover his birth date, parents' names, occupation, whether he can read and write and even a physical description. The description of his military status may also provide some valuable genealogical information. For example, a young man could be declared ineligible for service because he was the oldest son and his father was dead. Thus, he was responsible for supporting his family.

Unfortunately, very few military records have been microfilmed by the Family History Library at this time. You will probably have to write to Italy to obtain this information. Chapter nine (Where to Find the Records), along with Appendix B (Letter-Writing Guide), will show you how to do this.

Books of Italian Surnames

If all other resources have failed to provide you with the town of your ancestor, one last resort is worth a try. There are books of Italian surnames that present the meaning and geographical origins of each name and its derivations. If your Italian surname is relatively uncommon, this source may help you narrow down your ancestral town to a few areas. One example of such a publication is *Our Italian Surnames*, by Joseph G. Fucilla (Genealogical Publishing Company, Baltimore, 1993).

Italian phone books can also provide the same information for the modern locations of people with your surnames. You may even find some living distant relatives! You can find Italian phone books in major libraries and the Family History Library (on microfilm). You can also purchase individual phone books from AT&T. Their free catalog lists all their domestic and international telephone directories, along with the price. Contact them at (800) 544-4988, extension 288.

Once you have identified the Italian hometown of your immigrant ancestor, you are ready to climb your family tree using the Italian vital records. The rest of this book provides the practical information that you need to perform this rewarding task.

SECTION III

The Records

CHAPTER SIX

Stato Civile: *Vital Records*

The civil vital records of Italy are amazingly comprehensive. These documents record births, marriages and deaths starting from about 1809 for most of Italy. For some areas, particularly in the south, the records are complete through today. Other areas may have gaps due to political changes or natural loss, such as fire or flood. From about 1865, the time of Italy's last unification, vital records exist throughout Italy.

Some Disadvantages and How to Overcome Them

The *Stato Civile* are some of the easiest genealogical records to use. They were specifically designed for future referencing, so they are blessed with many useful features of which we can take advantage. Of course, there are also a few disadvantages that can make them difficult to use. Let's take a look at these disadvantages first.

The Language Barrier

Obviously, these records are not written in English. This fact alone stops many people from even attempting to use the records because they fear the foreign language. Actually, anyone can easily learn to understand the *Stato Civile*.

Italian is a not a difficult language, and anyone who has ever studied any language sharing its common Latin roots, such as Spanish or French, will be surprised at the similarities. For example, the number five in Italian is *cinque*, which is spelled almost the same way in French (cinq) although it is pronounced much differently. If you have ever studied another language you will have an advantage here.

Even if you know only English, you will have little trouble reading Italian vital records. After all, we are not talking about reading the original version of Dante's *Divine Comedy*, but merely some basic genealogical documents such as birth and marriage records. There are only a handful of words and phrases that you need to know in order to understand the *Stato Civile*. Learn the basic vocabulary, such as numbers, months, relationships and so forth, and you can read Italian vital records. And once you've mastered these basics, they are yours forever.

Appendix A contains Italian word lists of genealogical value to assist you in reading Italian vital records. You may also wish to invest in an Italian/English dictionary for an occasional unusual occupation. Throughout this book there are many examples of Italian vital records, transcribed and translated, to help you learn how to read and understand these documents.

Undecipherable Records

The first time I read an old Italian birth record, it was like trying to understand an optometrist's eye chart. Even if it were written in English, I would have had trouble deciphering it! There are two reasons for this.

First, some letters were written differently in the nineteenth century. For example, the lowercase *s* was frequently written like the lowercase *f*. This can confuse the novice. However, after struggling to decipher many documents, I learned how each letter was written and which letters could be ambiguous. Then I was able to read nineteenth-century handwriting without even thinking about it.

You won't have to struggle to get to this point though. Just read chapter seven, which includes a section on deciphering old style handwriting and shows examples of some of the more commonly confused letters. Then practice your paleography (the study of ancient handwriting) skills by reading the actual document examples throughout this book.

The second reason for the difficulty in deciphering some of these old documents involves their legibility. The record keepers used fountain pens or even quills which could be scratchy and often dripped blobs of ink or left smears. Also, the records are very old and may have faded with time or been damaged by insects, mildew or dirt. One way to overcome this problem is by taking advantage of the redundancy that occurs in Italian documents. As you will see when we review some actual records, the same information may appear several times throughout a single document. For example, the name of the baby in a birth record appears in the index, in the body of the document and in the baptism section. If it is illegible in one place, look for it in another.

Advantages of the *Stato Civile*

Now you are aware of the two disadvantages in using the *Stato Civile* and you know tactics to overcome them. Now let's look at the advantages of these records because, as you will see, they far outweigh the disadvantages.

They Exist!

The Italians have always been great record keepers and have preserved their records for all these years. The Family History Library has many of these documents on microfilm and makes them readily available to everyone. It always amazes me that I can find the 1814 birth record of my fifth great-grandmother from some little known Italian town, all while sitting in the comfort of my local Family History Center. It seems miraculous, but these records are out there just waiting for you!

They are Consistent

Unlike church records, which vary with the styles of the priests, the structure of the vital records was defined by Napoleon when he unified Italy. This basic format has been retained throughout the existence of the vital records. Most of the records were created in books of preprinted forms. All the clerk had to do was fill in the blanks, making them very easy to read.

You may find some documents written entirely in free format. There were no preprinted forms available for some of the years, or maybe they ran out of forms at the end of the year because there were more births or deaths than anticipated. Sometimes the books of forms did not arrive in the town until after the beginning of the year. In these cases, the records may require a little more effort to understand, but even these followed a standard boilerplate phraseology that mimicked the preprinted forms.

Because of this consistency, Italian vital records are very easy to use. Once you have learned to read one birth record, you can read them all.

They Are Indexed

Almost all the *Stato Civile* have an annual index, created by the local clerk at the end of each year. These indices are real time-savers. It is much quicker to read a few pages of an index than hundreds of pages of records.

These indices usually include the parents' names in addition to the name of the baby (for birth records), bride and groom (for marriage records) and the deceased (for death records). This allows you to search very quickly for siblings and other relatives.

Chapter seven will provide more detailed information about how to use these valuable indices.

They Include Margin Notations

Margin notations are references appended to the margins of the vital records, usually birth records. These notations may contain information about the child's marriage and sometimes his or her death. These act as great confirming and cross-referencing aids. For example, the birth record of my great-great-grandfather, Pasquale Luisi, contains a margin notation stating that he married Rosa Quartodipalo in Gravina on April 19, 1887. Since I knew that was his wife's name, this piece of information confirmed that I had the correct Pasquale Luisi and not one of his many cousins. Also, I essentially had no information about his wife, Rosa, at the time, so this margin notation allowed me to find their marriage record and learn all about Rosa's family. You can see how these margin notations can be treasure chests of information. We will review some actual examples later on.

They Note Women's Maiden Names

One of the greatest advantages of Italian documents is that women are always referenced by their maiden names. Birth records list the mother by her maiden name. Marriage documents reference the mothers of both the bride and groom by their maiden names. Even death records use the woman's maiden name and only specify her married name when mentioning her husband. Anyone who has ever spent months or years trying to determine the maiden name of an American ancestor will really appreciate this.

All these great advantages of the *Stato Civile* contribute to the records' usefulness. You shouldn't fear these records. Their accessibility often makes Italian records easier to use than North American documents. Now, let's cover some tips and tricks for using the *Stato Civile*.

CHAPTER SEVEN

The Best Tips for Using the Stato Civile

An inexperienced researcher working with the vital records of Italy can encounter many unfamiliar and frustrating problems, such as strange handwriting, words that can't be translated and things that just don't make sense. This chapter offers information that is usually learned the hard way, through experience. These tips will immediately make you more comfortable with the *Stato Civile*.

Old Style Handwriting

The handwriting style of the eighteenth and nineteenth centuries is a bit different from the current style. If you have experience in reading any documents of this period (not just Italian ones) you are familiar with this already. For example, the American Declaration of Independence is in a style similar to what you will find in the *Stato Civile*. The following tips will help you interpret that handwriting.

The Italian Alphabet

The Italian alphabet is slightly different than the English alphabet. True Italian does not contain the following letters:

J   K   W   X   Y

You may find some words containing these letters in modern Italian. For example, the word *whiskey*, which uses three of these letters, is in Italian dictionaries. However, this is an English word that has been brought into modern Italian. You will never find these letters in the nineteenth century documents of the *Stato Civile* except in certain dialects.

Knowing this fact will be very useful in your research. For example, if you're trying to decipher a word in an 1823 death record and are not quite sure if a certain letter is a *y* or a *g*, you can immediately eliminate the possibility of it being a *y*.

The Lowercase *s*

The lowercase *s* of the nineteenth century is one of the more commonly confused letters because it resembles lowercase *f*. The following examples illustrate this:

Francesco	Francesco
nascita	nascita
sessanta	sessanta
sessanta	sessanta

Usually, when a word contains a double *s*, the first one will be the long *s* and the second will be the short *s* that we use today. However, this is not always the case as shown in the two different examples of the word *sessanta*.

The Uppercase *R*

The uppercase *R* can cause a lot of headaches, as you can see in the examples on page 38. It often resembles the uppercase *V*, sometimes looks like an uppercase *B*, and may even be completely ambiguous. Of course, it may also look like an *R*.

The first *Rosa* can confuse the inexperienced

researcher since it contains both the *R* and *s*. To the uninitiated, it looks like *Vofa*!

	Rosa
	Rosina
	Rosa
	Rosa

Uppercase *D, F, G, I* and *T*
These uppercase letters are frequently confused with each other.

	Tommaso
	Trenta
	Filippo
	Francesco

There are two things to do if you are not sure which letter you are reading. First, use the rest of the word and its context to determine which letter would make the most sense. For example, the leading *T* in the word *Trenta* (thirty) above is ambiguous. Seeing that it is followed by *renta* and that the entire word follows the word *anni* (years), we can narrow it down to a number, in this case, *trenta*.

The second trick to try in a case like this is to compare the unknown letter to similar letters in known words within the same document, because the person writing the document probably used the letters consistently. If you suspect the letter is *F*, then compare it to the *F* in a known word. For example, if the document was recorded in the province of Foggia, you will find the word Foggia in the document. Compare this *F* to your suspected *F*.

Uppercase *L, P* and *S*
These letters may be easily confused for each other, as shown here.

	Palo
	Savino
	Pasqua
	Leopoldo

Use the same methods described above to assist you in understanding these letters.

Lowercase *i* Resembles Lowercase *j*
The lowercase *i* may look exactly like the lowercase *j*, as shown in these examples.

Remember, there is no *j* in true Italian. Therefore, it must be an *i*.

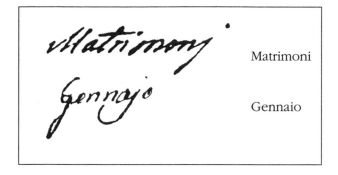

Matrimoni	Matrimoni
Gennaio	Gennaio

	di
	di
	deciotto
	della

Lowercase Loop Letters, *p, g, q* and *z*

These must sometimes be interpreted solely by their context within the rest of the word and the rest of the sentence, as shown here.

	quaranta
	propriatario
	figlio
	opposizione

Lowercase *d*

The lowercase *d* is used frequently in vital records (in the word *di* for example). As a result, it is sometimes written in an almost shorthand fashion, as shown here.

Numbers

Although numbers were usually written out as words, you will find the digits used to reference page or record numbers. *7* and *1* are easily confused, as are *7* and *2*. *5* is often ambiguous.

The nineteenth-century handwriting style at first might frighten you. However, after reading a few

	2
	3
	4
	16
	17
	29
	31
	34
	47
	49
	50
	127

documents, you will come to interpret these odd letters without even blinking. Practice this skill by reading the sample documents in this book.

Abbreviations

The clerks creating the *Stato Civile* spent a lot of time writing. They often had to squeeze quite a bit of information into a small space, especially in the indices and margins. Consequently, they used abbreviations frequently. To the inexperienced researcher these may seem undecipherable. Even worse, they could cause incorrect translations. Below are some of the more common abbreviations that you will find while researching Italian vital records.

First Names

First names were frequently abbreviated, particularly in the indices. Generally, the first syllable was written normally with the last syllable following it in superscript, as shown in these examples.

- Ant^o = Antonio
- Arc^a = Arcangela
- Dom^{co} = Domenico
- Em^{le} = Emanuelle
- $Fran^{co}$ = Francesco
- $Gius^e$ = Giuseppe
- M^a = Maria
- Vin^{za} = Vincenza
- $Vitt^o$ = Vittorio

Titles

Titles of respect, such as *Dòn* or *Signóre* are also frequently abbreviated.

- D = *Dòn, Dònna* (Sir or Madam)
- D^a = *Dònna* (Madam, Lady)
- S^r = *Signóre* (Sir, Mister)
- S^{ra} = *Signóra* (Madam, Misses)

Months

The month portions of dates were often abbreviated in the indices. Many of them make sense, such as *feb°* for *febbràio*. Months are not capitalized in Italian.

However, there is one method of abbreviating

months that could cause great confusion until its secret is known. The months of September through December are frequently abbreviated as follows:

- 7bre = *settèmbre* (September)
- 8bre = *ottóbre* (October)
- 9bre = *novèmbre* (November)
- Xbre = *dicèmbre* (December)

If you were unaware of these abbreviations, you might assume the *7bre* meant the seventh month, July, instead of September; *8bre* meant the eighth month, August, instead of October; etc. You would be very wrong in this assumption and may suffer a lot of frustration in trying to find the document in the wrong month.

A little history will clarify this odd method of abbreviation. The Julian calendar, which was used until the mid-1500s throughout most of Europe, started its year with March. March was the first month, April the second, May the third, and so on. If you follow this through, September would be the seventh month, October the eighth, November the ninth, and December the tenth (the *X* in *Xbre* is the Roman numeral 10). These months' names in Italian begin with the number describing the month's original position in the Julian calendar. In Italian, *sètte* is seven, *òtto* is eight, *nòve* is nine and *dièci* is ten.

If you know a little Latin, you will see that even the English names for these months follow the same pattern. *Sept* is Latin for seven, *oct* is Latin for eight, and so on.

Ordinal Numbers

You may find ordinal numbers (first, second, etc.) abbreviated in the following fashion.

- 1^0 = *primo* (first)
- 4^0 = *quarto* (fourth)
- 7^0 = *sèttimo* (seventh)

Miscellaneous Abbreviations

You will frequently find the following two examples in the indices. They are used to indicate that the information is the same as the line above. For example, in an index for death records there is a column for place of birth. Since most individuals were born and died in the same town, the clerk would use an abbreviation to indicate this.

- *id = idem* (ditto)
- *d° = detto* (stated)

Word Continuations

When a word cannot fit completely on the end of a line of writing, it is continued on the next line. There is usually no indication that it is continued, although sometimes there may be a tiny underscore (_) at the end of the line. The word may be split anywhere, not just between syllables. Even proper names are treated this way. If you ever get stuck trying to translate a word that you cannot find in any dictionary, and that word starts on a new line, it may be the continuation of the previous word. Try putting the two pieces together and you just might solve the problem.

Interpreting Colloquialisms and Idioms

There are some words and phrases found in Italian vital records that, if translated literally, do not make sense. These idiomatic expressions must be understood in their context to be useful.

When reading the *Stato Civile*, we are not just reading a different language, but looking at a record of another culture from a different historical perspective. The examples below should clarify some of the unusual phrases you will find in these records.

Terms for the Deceased

The vital records always indicate whether a person is alive or dead. For example, in a marriage document the groom may be referenced as "Filippo, son of the late Nicola," indicating that his father was deceased at the time of Filippo's marriage.

This is a great benefit to ancestor hunters. It narrows down the range of possible years of a person's death, so when we look for a death record, we don't have to search as many years. For example, if the above Filippo was married in 1869 (and his father was deceased at that time) and Filippo's sister, "Maria, daughter of Nicola," was married in 1863,

we know that Nicola died sometime between 1863 and 1869.

Understanding the terms used to indicate the deceased is important. The possible expressions you will find in the *Stato Civile* are described here.

The most common word used to indicate death is "fu." The word *fu* literally means *was*, but when used in this context indicates that the person is deceased. All of the expressions below indicate that Filippo Calia is the son of the late Nicola and the living Rosa Luisi. Note that the words for *son* and *of* may be omitted and the word *fu* simply used alone.

- *Filippo Calia figlio del fu Nicola e di Rosa Luisi*
- *Filippo Calia del fu Nicola e di Rosa Luisi*
- *Filippo Calia fu Nicola e di Rosa Luisi*

If both parents are dead, *furono*, the plural form of the word, is used. All of the expressions below indicate that Filippo Calia is the son of Nicola Calia and Rosa Luisi, both of whom are deceased.

- *Filippo Calia figlio dei furono Nicola e Rosa Luisi*
- *Filippo Calia dei furono Nicola e Rosa Luisi*
- *Filippo Calia furono Nicola e Rosa Luisi*

Some examples of other expressions indicating a status of deceased are shown below.

- *Francesco, defunto*
- *Maria, defunta*
- *decèsso Francesco*
- *già Vincenza*

The Word *Di*

The word *di* (of) in Italian has many variations, depending on the number and gender of the word that follows it, as shown below.

- *del, dello, dell'* - masculine singular
- *dei, degli, degl'* - masculine plural
- *della, dell'* - feminine singular
- *delle* - feminine plural

Di (and all of its variations) can mean different things depending on the context. In Italian vital records you will find that when *di* follows a proper name it may be translated in one of four possible ways.

1. It is part of the surname (Giuseppe Di Maggio)
2. It indicates the parent's name (Pietro di Francesco)
3. It indicates the birthplace (Vito di Bitonto)
4. It indicates the place of residence (Maria di Palo)

The trick is to know which one. Reading the rest of the document will help eliminate some possibilities. For example, if later in the sentence it states, *nato in Modugno* (born in Modugno), then you know that the *di* cannot indicate the birthplace. If you read, *figlio di Pasquale* (son of Pasquale), then you know it doesn't indicate the name of the father. If you find *domiciliata in Palo* (residing in Palo), then the *di* cannot refer to the place of residence.

Familiarity with Italian first names and the names of other towns in the province will also assist you in making this distinction. Appendix A (Italian Word Lists) contains lists of common Italian first names.

Written Numbers

You will notice that in the records of the *Stato Civile* almost all numbers for years, days and ages are written out as words. Instead of *21* you will see *ventuno*. Although this requires that you learn the Italian words for numbers, it is a benefit because there is little ambiguity with written numbers. For example, it is sometimes difficult to distinguish the digits *1* and *7*, but there is no confusion between *uno* and *sètte*.

See Appendix A for a complete word list of all numbers.

Dates and Time

Dates are usually written out, but occasionally, particularly in more recent documents, the date may be abbreviated in a day/month/year format. For example, January 4, 1902, would be shown as 04/01/02. This is the European method which many North Americans incorrectly translate as April 1, 1902.

When recording the time of an event, such as a birth, the 24-hour clock is frequently used. If you are familiar with military time, you already understand this. One o'clock A.M. through noon are the hours one through twelve. One o'clock P.M. through midnight are hours thirteen through twenty-four. So *ore diciòtto* (eighteen hours) is 6:00 P.M.

Gender Distinction

English is one of the few languages that does not assign a gender to its inanimate nouns. In Italian, all nouns are either masculine or feminine, and the words that modify them (adjectives and verbs) must use the appropriate gender format. Although this concept is foreign to English readers, it is important to understand because it can help you clarify ambiguities in your research.

For example, you are translating a death record and the first name is either Mario or Maria, but the handwriting makes it difficult to distinguish. Look at the verbs used for this person and see whether they are masculine or feminine. Generally, verbs modifying feminine subjects end in *a*, while verbs modifying masculine subjects end in *o*. Does the death record read *mòrto* or *mòrta* (died)? For the place of birth, does it say *nato* or *nata*? You can use this technique to clarify the gender of any person mentioned in an Italian vital record.

Titles

Although most of the people you find in the vital records will not have a title, sometimes you will see a title of some sort before a name. The most common ones are *Dòn* (for men) and *Dònna* (for women). It is important to recognize that this is not the first name of the person. Nor does it necessarily mean that they are of noble blood. It may simply be a title of respect for a high-standing member of the community. Some titles that you will see are as follows:

- *Dòn* - Sir (abbreviated *D*)
- *Dònna* - Madam, Lady (abbreviated *D* or *D*ᵃ)
- *Signóre* - Sir, Mr. (abbreviated *S*ʳ)
- *Signóra* - Madam, Mrs. (abbreviated *S*ʳᵃ)
- *Maèstro* - Master, teacher

Utilizing the Indices

Almost every year of Italian births, marriages and deaths is indexed, so hunting for a specific ancestor, or even a family name is quick and easy. Each year has its own index, so you should always find the index first when reviewing vital records for a particular year. Since Italians frequently need to obtain extracts of vital records for various reasons (to get married, for military conscription, etc.), the records were indexed to make this process easy for the clerks, but it has been a great benefit to genealogical researchers as well!

On the microfilm, the index is generally located just prior to the records or immediately following them. Sometimes, if the records required a second book, there may be a second or even third index for one year. This is particularly true of death records in epidemic years. Make sure you find and search them all.

The indices are arranged roughly in alphabetical order by the first letter of the name of the baby (for birth records), groom (for marriage records), or the deceased (for death records). Usually this sequence is based on the last name, although quite frequently, especially in the older records, the index is by first name. If you are searching for a specific ancestor, such as Paolo Mondello, it really shouldn't matter which way the index is sorted; you will look under the *P*s if it is by first name or the *M*s if it is by last name. If you are searching for the family name Vivaldi, however, you will have to look through the entire index if it is sorted by first name. This is still no great hardship, because searching through a dozen pages of index is much better than searching through hundreds of pages of documents.

These indices were generally created after the year was over. The clerk would start with the letter *A* and search chronologically through all the documents for that year, find a document with the name beginning with *A*, and extract the information into the index. When he was finished with the *A*s, he would index the *B*s and so on, through the alphabet. This means that within a single letter, the index is usually in chronological order, January through December.

Sometimes, the clerk would create the index when creating the records. He would leave spaces in the index under each letter for future records. If his estimate of the amount of space needed was wrong, you may find some names that wouldn't fit under the appropriate letter located at the end of the index. Less frequently, you will find a true alphabetical index, sorted by the entire name. In any case, no matter how the index is arranged, it is an easy task to search it.

Information in the Indices

The indices can contain an amazing amount of information. Birth indices usually contain the name of the baby, the parents' names (including the mother's maiden name), the date of birth, and a reference number, which we will discuss in a moment. Marriage indices usually contain the names of the bride and groom, both of their parents' names (including the mothers' maiden names), the date of the marriage and a reference number. Death indices usually contain the name of the deceased, the parents' names (including the mother's maiden name), the date of death, often the birthplace and occupation, and the reference number. The wealth of information in the Italian records' indices alone is greater than what is found in the actual records of some other countries!

Index Reference Numbers

The reference number in the indices could be one of two things. Sometimes it references the page number or document number of the actual record, in which case you can just go directly to the record by using this reference number. More often, however, the number is just a sequential number assigned during the indexing process. You can easily tell which one of the two it represents by scanning a column of these numbers in the index. If they are consecutive in the index, we can assume that they are not page or document numbers (it is doubtful that the *bambini* would have been accommodating enough to be born in alphabetical order).

Using Index Dates

If the reference number is not the page or document number, but simply a sequential index number, you must use the date to help you find the actual document. The documents appear in the order in which they were created, not necessarily the order in which the event occurred. This is very important to understand. As you will learn when we discuss the actual records, births and deaths were generally recorded within a day or two after they occurred, but marriages were often recorded shortly before the event. You must understand this fact in order to use the date in the index to find the document.

If a birth index lists the birth date as September 7, then you must find the first record with September 7 as the recording date and start looking from that date forward. The birth may have been recorded on the seventh, eighth, ninth or tenth of September. I have even seen births recorded as late as two weeks after they occurred. Use the same process for death records. You shouldn't have to go more than a day beyond the death date.

For marriage indices, you will usually reverse the process since the marriage was usually recorded prior to the actual event. If the marriage date was September 7, then find the last record with the recording date of September 7 and look from that record backwards. Since the marriage was usually recorded shortly before the actual event, the document may have been recorded on the seventh, sixth, fifth, etc.

If you find an index entry but have trouble finding the actual document, then try looking several days before and after the date listed in the index.

Example of Birth Record Index

Let's look at some actual indices of Italian vital records.

Figure 7-9 is an index page for birth records. The first column, *Numero d'ordine*, shows the reference number. In scanning this column of numbers we see that the numbers are not consecutive, they jump around. This indicates that the reference number represents a page or document number. Once we find the entry in this index, finding the actual document will be a simple matter of finding the page or document with the same reference number.

The next column, *Cognomi, e Nomi dei Nati*, contains the surname and given name of the newborn. In reviewing this column of information, we see that it is sorted by last name. For example, the first entry is *Cali Filippo*. This means that we can go right to the alphabetical section for the surname in which we are interested. This particular sample page contains the letters *C*, *E* and *F*. Oddly, the letter *D* appears to be missing. Because last names beginning with *D* are fairly common in Italian, it would appear that the indexer accidentally skipped this letter. If I were searching for a name beginning with *D*, I would check the end of the index, hoping that the indexer discovered his omission and added it to the end.

The third column, *Cognomi, e Nomi dei Genitori*, contains the names of the parents of the newborn. The fathers' first names only are listed here because their last names are the same as those of the babies. Both the mothers' maiden names and first names are listed here. For example, the parents' names for the first entry are *Salvatore e Panzica Rosaria*. The mother's maiden name is listed first in this example.

The last column, *Giorno della Nascita*, contains the day of birth. Only the day and month are written here because the year is assumed to be the same for the entire index. Some of the entries use the abbreviations discussed earlier, such as the first entry reading *11 9bre*, which indicates the eleventh of November.

Birth indices, like this one, make it very easy to find the birth records of your ancestors. Although this is a typical example, you will find some variations. For example, sometimes only the father's name will appear in the index. No matter what the format of the index, you should always take advantage of this aid.

Example of Marriage Record Index

Figure 7-10 shows a page from a typical marriage index. This index is from a supplement, that is, all the marriage records for this year (1830) did not fit in a single book, so they were continued in a second book.

The first column, *Num. d'ordine*, is the reference number. This index starts with number 71 because it is the index for the supplement. Because they continue consecutively down the page, we know

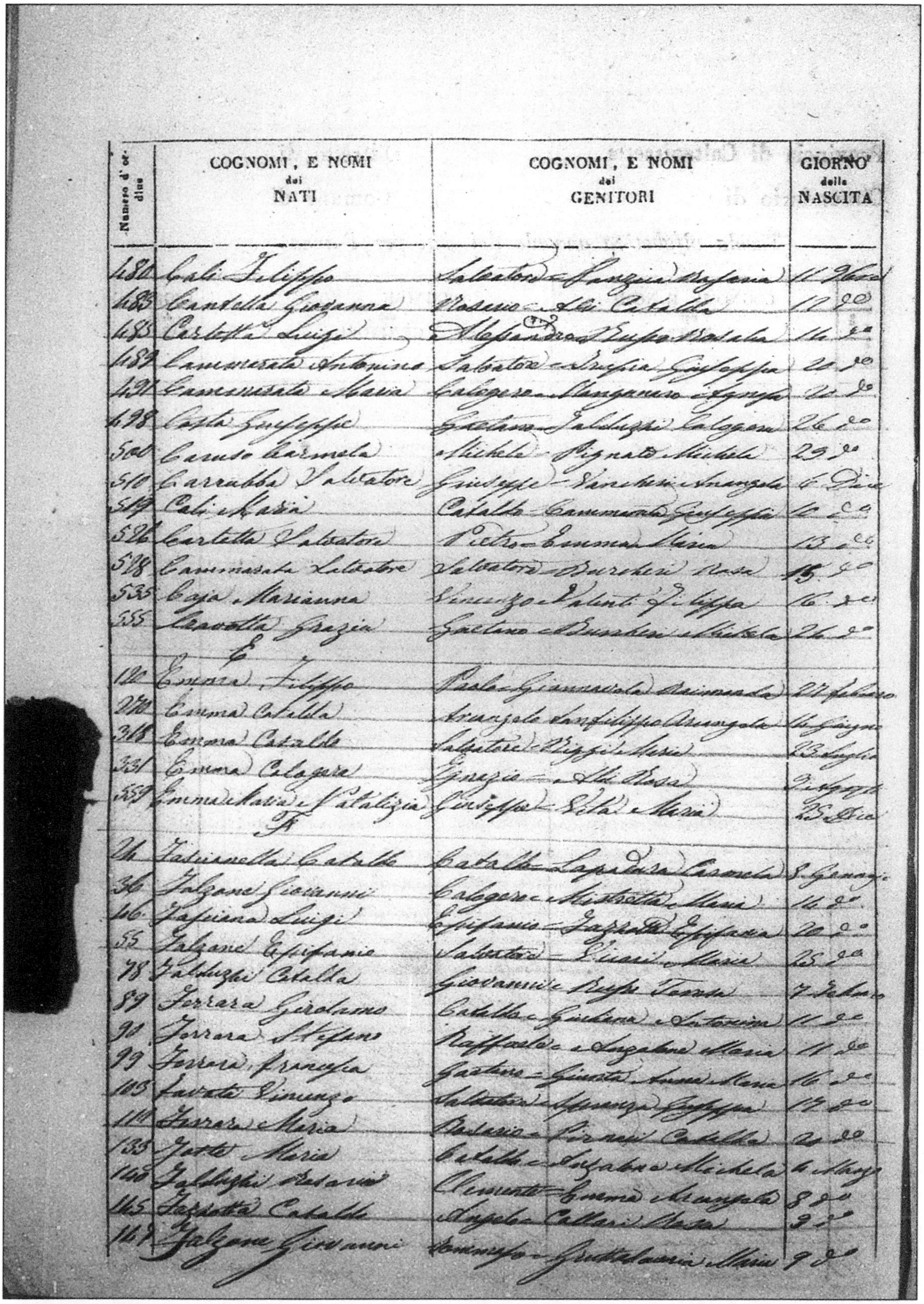

FIGURE 7-9 **Typical index page for birth records. (Photograph courtesy of the Family History Library of The Church of Jesus Christ of Latter-day Saints)**

Num. d' ordine	COGNOMI, e NOMI degli Sposi	PATRIA	COGNOMI, e NOMI de' Genitori.	Giorno della celebrazione del matrimonio innanzi alla Chiesa	Osservazioni
	B.			1830	
71	*Braja Carlo* *Riccio della Maria*				
	C.				
72					
73					
74					
75					
76					
	D.				
77					
	F.				
78					
79					
	G.				
80					
	L.				
81	*Lombardi*				

FIGURE 7-10 **Typical index page for marriage records. (Photograph courtesy of the Family History Library of The Church of Jesus Christ of Latter-day Saints)**

that the reference numbers are not page or document numbers, which means we must use the date of marriage to locate the actual marriage document.

The next column, *Cognomi, e Nomi degli Sposi*, contains the surnames and given names of the newlyweds. Each entry contains the groom's surname and given name and then the bride's surname and given name, slightly indented. For example, number 80 lists the groom as Gramegna Mich[e] and the bride as Nardone Fran[ca]. Note how the first names are abbreviated in the typical manner discussed earlier. Because this index is sorted by last name, we should go directly to the section containing the last names beginning with the letter of the name for which we are searching.

Column three, *Patria*, indicates the birthplaces of the newlyweds. The lowercase *i* for some entries is an abbreviation for *idem* (ditto). These records were created in the town of Gravina. Notice how almost all the brides were born in Gravina, while many of the grooms were from other towns. Numbers 72 and 74 were born in Altamura, number 76 is from Santeramo and number 81 was born in Bari. This is evidence of the common custom of the marriage taking place in the hometown of the bride.

The next column, *Cognomi, e Nomi de'Genitori*, lists the surnames and given names of the parents of the newlyweds. Only the first name of the father is written, since his last name is the same as his child, the bride or groom. The mother's first name and maiden name are also shown here. The writing in this column is small and cramped. If you have trouble reading some of these names, remember, they will be listed again in the actual document.

The fifth column, *Giorno della celebrazione del matrimonio innanzi alla Chiesa*, indicates the date of the church marriage ceremony. Generally, the year is not given since the entire index is for the same year. In this example the clerk entered the year, 1830, at the top of the column. The day number and an abbreviation for the month are shown. For example, number 71 shows 16 Nov[e] (November) as the marriage date. You would use this date to find the actual record because the reference number in the first column is just a sequential index number.

The last column, *Osservazioni*, is for notes. I've never seen this column used.

You can see that this index contains a wealth of information. It also makes it easy to search for any siblings or other relatives—simply scan through the index looking for the same last name. You can scan the column containing the brides' and grooms' last names, and even the column showing the maiden names of the mothers.

This is a fairly typical example of a marriage index; however, some other variations exist. For example, you may find indices that list only the groom, or do not include all parents' names. In any case, the index is a great aid and time saver in your research.

Example of Death Record Index

Figure 7-11 shows an index page for death records. The first column, *N, D'Ordine*, is the reference number. Because the reference numbers continue consecutively down the page, we know that they are not page or document numbers, so we must use the date of death to help us locate the actual death record.

The second column contains the names of the deceased. By reading these names we see that in this example, the index is sorted on first name (number 109 is Gius[e], number 115 is Laura, etc.). If we were looking for Luca Mercurio, we would look through the *L* section. On this page there are two Luca Mercurios, numbers 117 and 119.

The third column, *Patria*, indicates the place of birth of the deceased. Notice the word *idem* (ditto) is used to show that the place of birth is the same as the one above. *Idem* is not the name of a town. The first entry in this column states Palo as the birthplace.

The fourth column shows the occupation of the deceased. Note the abbreviation of the word *contadino* on line number 111. The lines with a blank occupation are probably children; the actual record will provide the age at death.

Column five, *Cognomi e Nomi de'Genitori*, indicates the names of the parents of the deceased. We can use this to determine if one of the two Luca Mercurios is the one we are researching. The father's first name only is presented because his last name is the same as his child's, the deceased. The

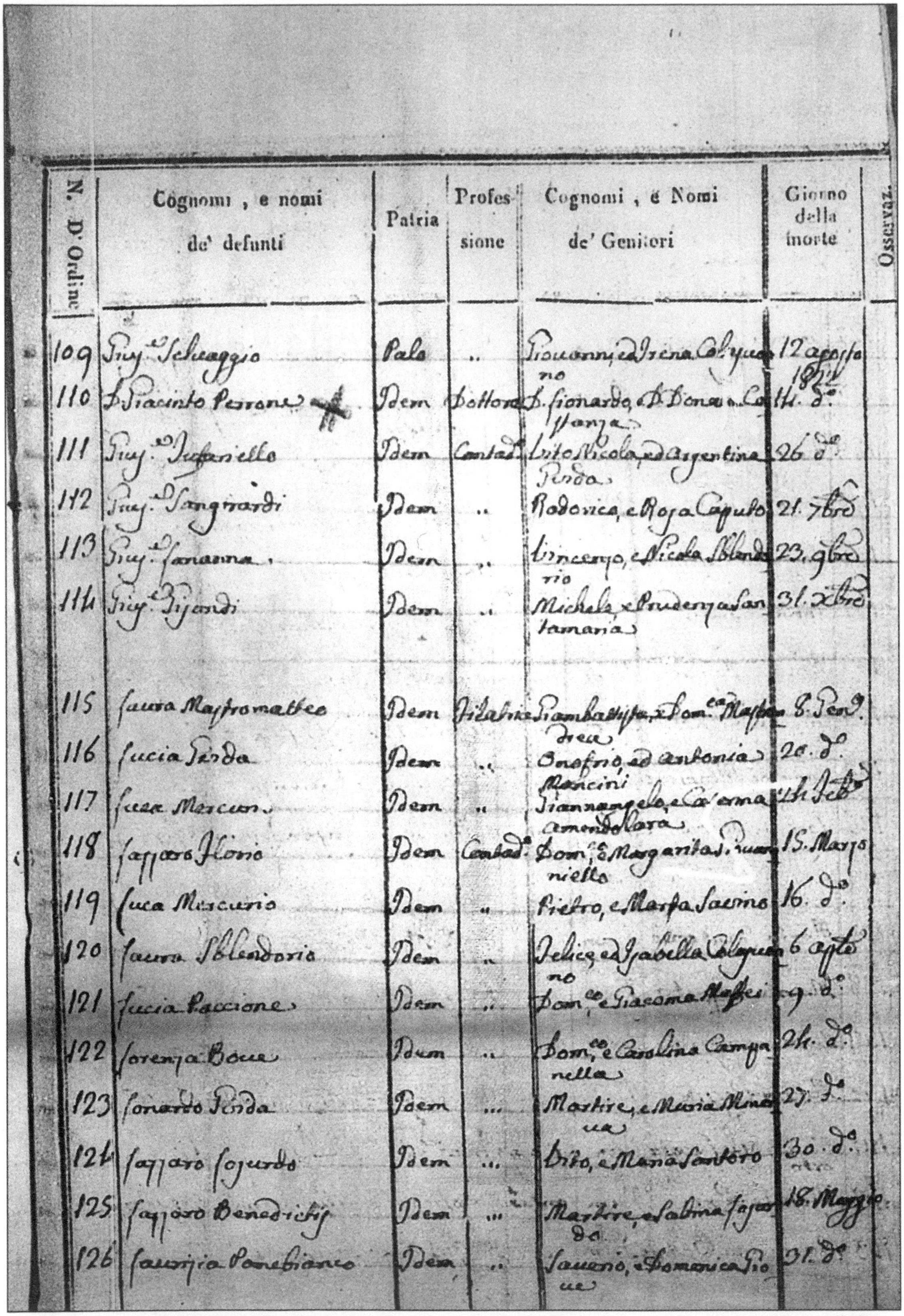

N. D'Ordine	Cognomi, e nomi de' defunti	Patria	Professione	Cognomi, e Nomi de' Genitori	Giorno della morte	Osservaz.
109	Giuse Selvaggio	Palo	..	Giovanni, ed Irena Colaquano	12 agosto 18[illegible]	
110	D. Giacinto Perrone	Idem	Dottore	D. Leonardo, e D. Dona [illegible] Costanza	14. do.	
111	Giuse [illegible]	Idem	Contad.	Vito Nicola, ed Argentina Penda	26 do.	
112	Giuse Sangirardi	Idem	..	Rodorica, e Rosa Caputo	21. 7bre	
113	Giuse [illegible]	Idem	..	Vincenzo, e Nicola Sblendorio	23. 9bre	
114	Giuse [illegible]	Idem	..	Michele, e Prudenza Santamaria	31. Xbre	
115	Laura Mastromatteo	Idem	Filatrice	Giambattista, e Dom.ca Massa [illegible]	8. Gen.o	
116	Lucia Penda	Idem	..	Onofrio, ed Antonia Mancini	20. do.	
117	Luca Mercurio	Idem	..	Giannangelo, e Carmina Amendolara	14 Feb.o	
118	Lazzaro Florio	Idem	Contad.	Dom.co, e Margarita [illegible]	15. Marzo	
119	Luca Mercurio	Idem	..	Pietro, e Marta Saerno	16. do.	
120	Laura Sblendorio	Idem	..	Felice, ed Isabella Colaquano	6 aple	
121	Lucia Paccione	Idem	..	Dom.co, e Giacoma Massei	9. do.	
122	Lorenza Bove	Idem	..	Dom.co, e Carolina Campanella	24. do.	
123	Leonardo Penda	Idem	...	Martire, e Maria [illegible]	27. do.	
124	Lazzaro Lojurdo	Idem	...	Vito, e Maria Santoro	30. do.	
125	Lazzaro Benedictis	Idem	...	Martire, e Sabina [illegible]	18. Maggio	
126	Laurizia Panebianco	Idem	..	Saverio, e Domenica Giove	31. do.	

FIGURE 7-11 **Typical index page for death records. (Photograph courtesy of the Family History Library of The Church of Jesus Christ of Latter-day Saints)**

mother's first name and maiden name are both given. In the index, there is usually no indication of whether the parent is alive or dead; you will find that information in the actual document. Notice how some of the mothers' maiden names will not fit on one line and are simply continued below. There is a tiny underscore (_) beneath the last letter on the first line to indicate that the name is continued.

The last column gives the date of death. Since this index is for a particular year, the year is usually not written in the index, although in this example the clerk wrote the year with the first date on each page. Number 109 shows the date of 12 *agósto* 1822. The months are abbreviated, as discussed earlier in this chapter. For example, the date for number 112 is 21 *7bre* (September 21). The *d°* used for the months in numbers 110 and 111 is for "ditto," indicating that these months are the same as the one above, August. If you look at number 118 and are not sure if the month is *marzo* (March) or *màggio* (May), there is a trick to determine which one it is. Since the index is usually in chronological order within each letter, look at the last month above and the first month below the month in question. Since number 118 is preceded by *febbràio* and followed by *aprile*, we know that it cannot be *màggio* (May), and therefore must be *marzo* (March).

If we are looking for a specific person, such as Luca Mercurio, we simply go to the page containing the names beginning with *L*, since this index is sorted on the first name. If we were looking for any Mercurio, hoping to find Luca's siblings or other relatives, we would look through the entire index, scanning the column containing the name of the deceased for anyone named Mercurio. We could even search the column containing the mothers' maiden names to find Mercurios. You can see how the index is a valuable tool to help you quickly and easily find your ancestors.

Read Those Margin Notations

Margin notations are small paragraphs of handwritten text found in the margins of vital records, usually added years after the document was created. They generally served two purposes. Primarily, they

added new information about the person on the record. Less frequently, they corrected an error made on the original record. For researching your family history, they could be the key that unlocks a whole new branch of your family tree, so it is important that you read them.

Although you will not find them on all documents, the most common margin notation you will see is the marriage reference added to a birth record. This information was appended to the birth record at the time of the marriage, even if the marriage occurred in a different town. As shown in the example in Figure 7-12, it simply states the date, place and names of the bride and groom. Sometimes, as in this example, it will even give the document number.

For our purposes, this type of margin notation is the most useful. When you think that you have found the birth record of your great-great-grandfather, Giuseppe Angelastro, use the margin notation to confirm that this is your ancestor. You should already know his wife's name, so the margin notation will tell you if this is your Giuseppe Angelastro.

Occasionally, a birth record will be appended with death information. If the person died young, before they could have had any children, then you know that this person could not be your ancestor. If it is your ancestor, now you know their death date.

Less common margin notations are corrections to errors in the original document. For example, the birth record of my great-great-grandfather, Pasquale Luisi, contained a margin notation that changed his first name. The clerk who originally created the birth record accidentally wrote his name as Pasqua, the female version of Pasquale (they knew he was male, however, because the record stated *maschile*, for male). The margin notation, created fifteen years after the birth, stated that the name in the record could be officially changed from Pasqua to Pasquale because the baby was a male, not a female. After reading this, I noticed that *le* had been added to the name Pasqua in different handwriting.

Another example of this type of margin notation shows how critical these could be to your research. I was looking for the death record of my fourth

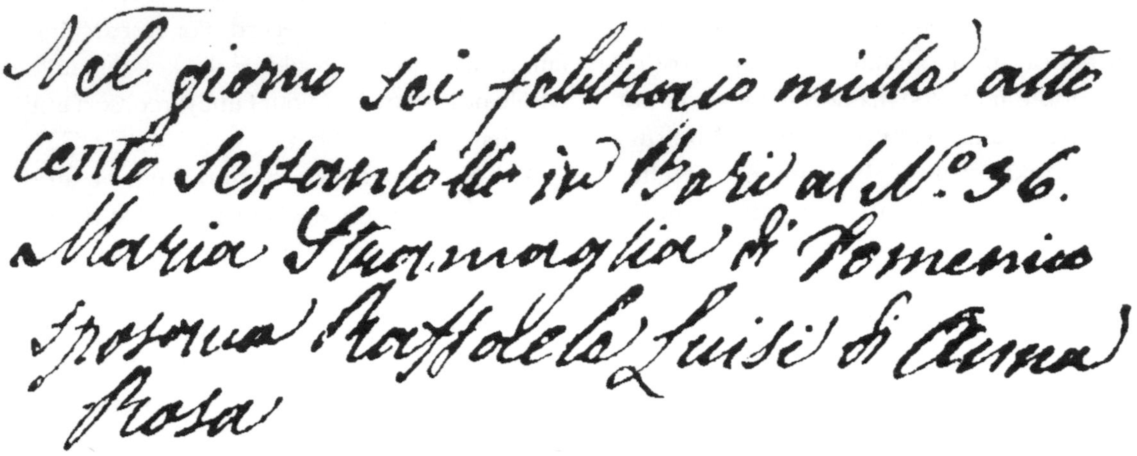

*Nel giorno sei febbraio mille otto
cento sessantotto in Bari al N.º 36.
Maria Stramaglia di Domenico
sposina Raffaele Luisi di Anna
Rosa*

*Nel giorno sei febbraio mille otto
cento sessantotto in Bari al N.º 36
Maria Stramaglia di Domenico
sposara Raffaele Luisi di Anna
Rosa*

On day six February one thousand eight
hundred sixty eight in Bari at number 36
Maria Stramaglia (dau) of Domenico
married Raffaele Luisi (son) of Anna
Rosa

FIGURE 7-12 **An example of a margin notation from a birth record, in original Italian handwriting, in typed Italian script and typed English.**

great-grandfather, Domenico Stramaglia, whose parents' names were unknown to me at that time because both his birth and marriage occurred before the initiation of the Napoleonic vital records. I found a record for a Domenico Stramaglia in the expected year and of the correct age, but it stated that his wife's name was Vittoria Pasqualicchio, not Vittoria Veloce, who was his wife (and my fourth great-grandmother). I was ready to pass this record by when I spotted a margin notation. This margin notation, written a year and a half after the death, corrected the name of the wife to Vittoria Veloce. I had found my fourth great-grandfather and discovered the next generation, his parents. Had I not read that margin notation, I would have missed that entire branch of the family forever.

These examples show how important margin notations can be in your research. Always seek them out and read them!

Taking Advantage of Redundancy

The Italian record keepers were almost obsessive in their recording of details. The political requirements of the times tried to satisfy both the church and state. As a result, there is a lot of redundancy in the Italian vital records. This is an advantage to genealogical researchers.

When we review some actual records you will see how the same information may be found several times throughout a single document. If a part of the document is damaged or illegible, you may find the same information in another area. For example, on a birth record, the father's name is found in the index, in the actual document and in the signature section. The baby's name is in the index, the body of the document and the baptism section of the document. The date of birth is found in the index and the document, the date of baptism is in the document and the date that the document was recorded is also in the document. These three dates, which are generally just days apart, may be used to clarify the month or day if there is any question about it.

There is similar redundancy in marriage records (and death records, to a lesser extent). Become familiar with the format and layout of typical Italian vital records (which we review in the next chapter).

Then when you find an unreadable word, instead of swearing, you know that you can find that information in another section of the document.

Secrets of Using an Italian/English Dictionary

Occasionally you may find a word that is not in any of the document examples in this guide or the word lists in Appendix A. For this reason you may wish to obtain an Italian/English dictionary.

Most words that you look up will give you a reasonable translation. Occasionally, however, you will find a translation that doesn't make sense. Usually it is because the meaning of the modern word is different than the meaning of the nineteenth-century word. For example, the occupation *vetturino* is a cab driver, according to my dictionary. Now our modern idea of a cab driver is a man in a yellow taxi. To clarify the definition, look up the English word in the English/Italian side of the dictionary. Cab driver has several definitions. The one for *vetturino* is clarified by the phrase "of a horse-drawn cab." Now it makes more sense.

Sometimes the translation between Italian and English is not quite accurate. An example of this is the Italian word *civile*. I found many ancestors with this occupation, but *civile* was not listed in any of the Italian occupation lists that I had collected over the years. The dictionary defined a *civile* as a civilian. Well, civilian has a military connotation, and there were no wars at this time. Also, many of the *civile* were women. I looked up the word civilian in the English/Italian side of the dictionary and found two definitions: *civile* and *borghese*. I then looked up *borghese* in the Italian/English side and it was defined as: bourgeois, person of the middle class, civilian. Well, now it makes more sense. These ancestors were members of the middle class. In old Italian, the word *civile* must have had several meanings but the dictionary only listed the more common modern usage.

Use this method of going back and forth between the Italian/English and English/Italian sides of the dictionary whenever you doubt the first translation.

Another good use for the dictionary is to learn the pronunciations of words. Usually, there is a table at the front of the book showing how each letter is pronounced. Of course, you really don't need to speak these words to do your research. However, as you read the Italian words in your head, you may as well be pronouncing them properly. Someday you may have discussions about some Italian words or phrases and you will sound more knowledgeable if you say them correctly.

Now that you know what peculiarities to expect from the *Stato Civile*, let's learn about the records themselves and review some actual examples.

CHAPTER EIGHT

The Records

Now we are ready to look at some actual examples of Italian *Stato Civile* (vital records). This chapter will describe the major Italian vital records that you will be using in your research and how they were created. The document samples provided here, with complete transcriptions and translations, will teach you how to read these records.

Atto di Nascita—Birth Record

Civil birth records in Italy were created in the *casa comunale* (town hall) by the officer of the vital records (usually the mayor of the town). The baby had to be physically present at the town hall in order to record the birth, so the birth was usually registered a day or two after the event.

The father of the baby was usually the informant (the person registering the birth), although frequently the midwife performed this service. In some towns during certain years, you will always find the midwife performing this service because it was considered part of her job. Occasionally another third party (such as a neighbor or relative) may have been the informant.

The clerk would record the date, time and place of the registration, along with the name, age, occupation and residence of the informant. The parents' names, ages, occupations and residence would also be noted. The birth information includes the date, time and place of birth as well as the baby's name and sex. Two witnesses were usually required and their names, ages, occupations and residences were also included. If any of the parties were able to write, they would sign their name at the end of the document.

Figures 8-1, 8-2 and 8-3 show the first page of the same birth record in three different formats. The first format is the original document. The second format replaces the handwritten Italian script with

typed Italian script, to assist in deciphering the handwriting. The third format replaces the Italian with English, showing how the document translates. For the rest of this discussion use the second and third formats for reference. Later, practice your translation skills by trying to read the first format on your own, using the second and third formats to assist you when you get stuck.

Figure 8-2, the first page of the birth record of Maria Stramaglia, is a typical example of an *Atto di Nascita*. Notice how the page is divided into two sections. The civil information is recorded in the body of the document (the left side) while the baptismal information is recorded in the right column.

The first section (A) of all birth records, and all records of the *Stato Civile*, is the same. It states the date and time that the registration occurred, not the date and time of the birth. Note that the numbers used in the date are written out as words and the use of the 24-hour clock (*seidici*, 16 hours is 4:00 P.M.). The name and title of the official recording the birth (usually the mayor in small towns) and the location (town, district and province) are also always included in this section.

The next section (B) includes information about the informant, the person registering the birth. The informant's name is given as Domenico Stramaglia fu Nicola, which indicates that Domenico is the son of the late Nicola. This is an important piece of genealogical information. The residence in this case simply states "in Bari," which is the name of the town. Sometimes you may see a street and even a house number.

The next section (C) states that he has presented *una femmina*. The word used here tells the sex of the baby. For females you may see the words *bambina*, *fanciulla*, *femminile*, *neonata* or *femmina*. For males you may see the words *bambino*,

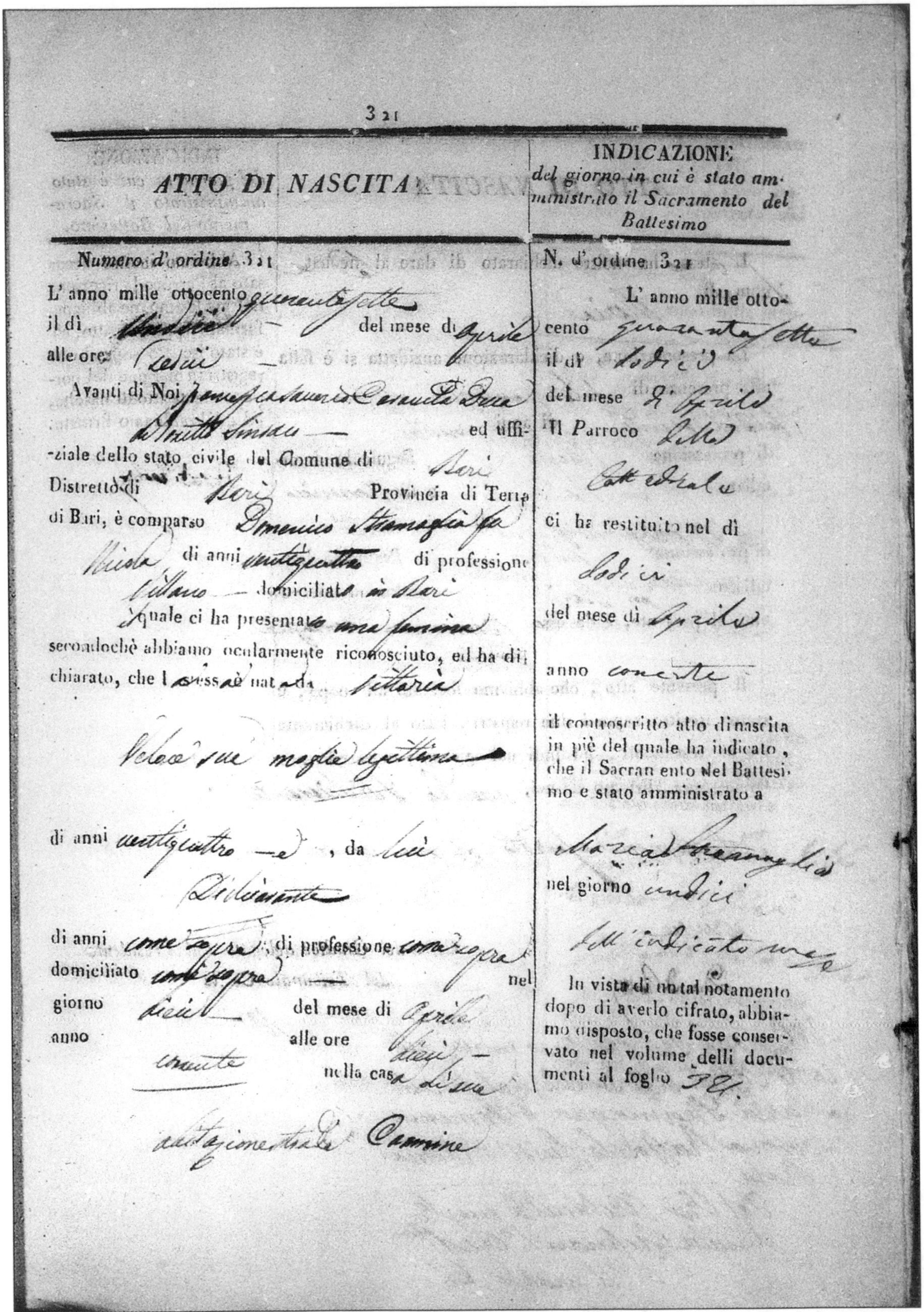

FIGURE 8-1 **1847 birth record of Maria Stramaglia, first page, original format. (Photograph courtesy of the Family History Library of The Church of Jesus Christ of Latter-day Saints)**

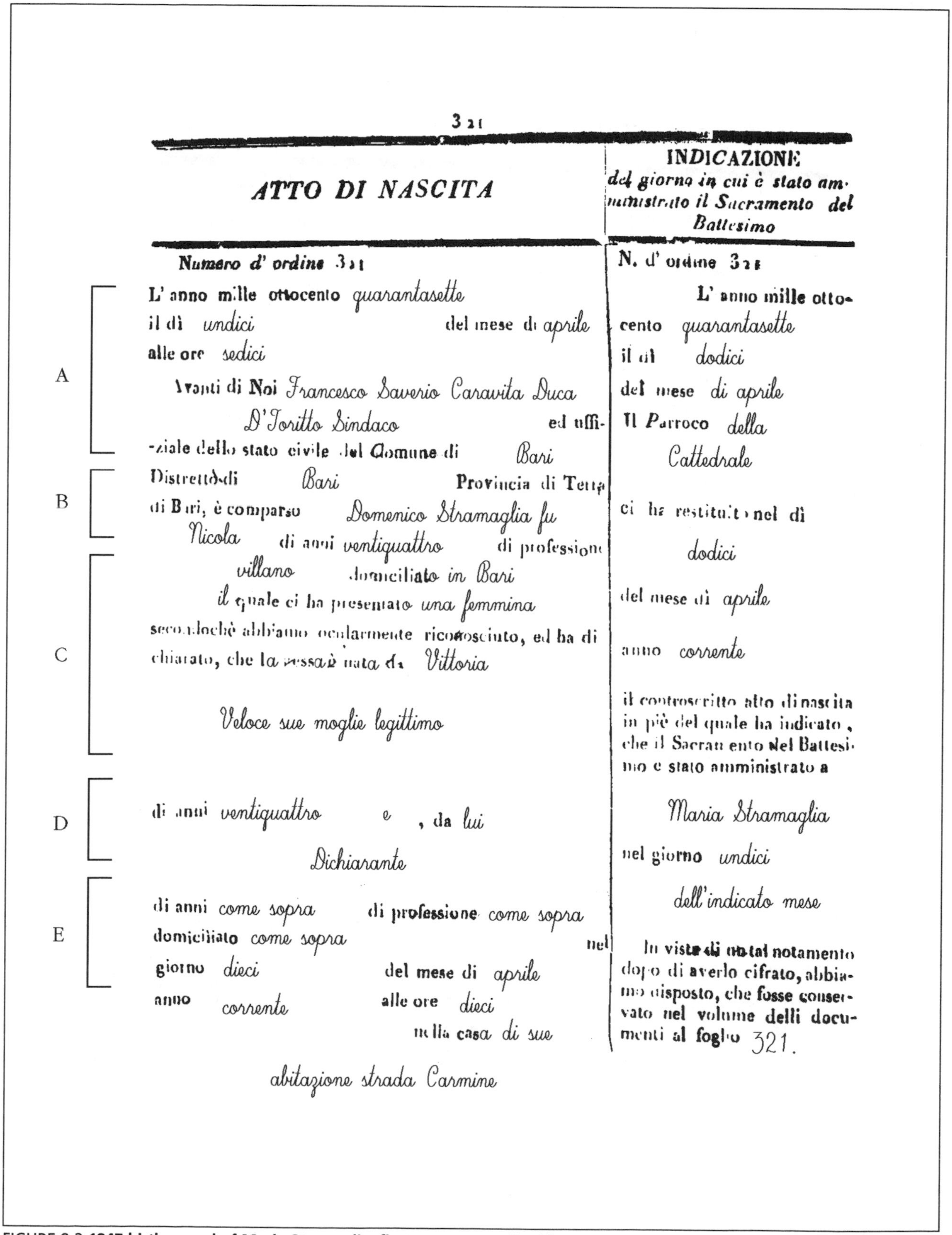

3 21

ATTO DI NASCITA	INDICAZIONE del giorno in cui è stato amministrato il Sacramento del Battesimo
Numero d' ordine 3 ı 1	N. d' ordine 3 ı ı

A
L' anno mille ottocento *quarantasette*
il dì *undici* del mese di *aprile*
alle ore *sedici*
Avanti di **Noi** *Francesco Saverio Caravita Duca*
D'Joritto Sindaco ed uffi-
ziale dello stato civile del Comune di *Bari*

B
Distretto di *Bari* **Provincia di Terra**
di B ıri, è comparso *Domenico Stramaglia fu*
Nicola di anni *ventiquattro* di professione

C
villano domiciliato in *Bari*
il quale ci ha presentato *una femmina*
secondoché abbiamo ocularmente riconosciuto, ed ha di
chiarato, che la sessa è nata da *Vittoria*

Veloce sua moglie legittimo

D
di anni *ventiquattro* e , da lui
Dichiarante

E
di anni *come sopra* di professione *come sopra*
domiciliato *come sopra* nel
giorno *dieci* del mese di *aprile*
anno *corrente* alle ore *dieci*
nella casa di sua
abitazione strada Carmine

L' anno mille otto-
cento *quarantasette*
il dì *dodici*
del mese di *aprile*
Il **P**arroco *della*
Cattedrale
ci ha restituito nel dì
dodici
del mese di *aprile*
anno *corrente*
il controscritto atto di nascita
in piè del quale ha indicato,
che il Sacramento del Battesi-
mo è stato amministrato a
Maria Stramaglia
nel giorno *undici*
dell'indicato mese
In vista di un tal notamento
dopo di averlo cifrato, abbiamo disposto, che fosse conser-
vato nel volume delli documenti al foglio *321.*

FIGURE 8-2 **1847 birth record of Maria Stramaglia, first page, transcribed format.**

3 21

BIRTH ACT

NOTICE
of the day on which was administered the Sacrament of
Baptism

Ordinal Number 321

In the year one thousand eight hundred *forty seven*
on day *eleven* of the month of *April*
at the hour *sixteen*

Before us *Francesco Saverio Caravita Duca*
D'Toritto Mayor — and offi-
cer of the Vital Records of the town of *Bari*
District of *Bari* Province of Terra
di Bari, appeared *Domenico Stramaglia son of the*
late Nicola age *twenty four* occupation
peasant living *in Bari*
the same has presented us *a female*
that we have visibly witnessed, and he has declared,
that the same was born of *Vittoria*

Veloce his legitimate wife

age *twenty four* and , of *him*

Informant

age *as above* occupation *as above*
living *as above* on the
day *ten* of the month of *Aprile*
year *current* at the hour of *ten*
in the house *of his*

dwelling Carmine Street

Ordinal No. 321

In the year one thousand eight
hundred *forty seven*
on day *twelve*
of the month *of April*
the rector *of the*
Cathedral

returned to us on day
twelve

of the month of *April*

year *current*

the here-written birth act
at the bottom of which he has indi‹
that the Sacrament of Baptism
was administered to

Maria Stramaglia

on day *eleven*
of the indicated month

Having seen this notice
after having it transcribed, we hav‹
arranged that it should be conserv‹
in the volume of documents
at page 321.

FIGURE 8-3 **1847 birth record of Maria Stramaglia, first page, translated format.**

fanciullo, neonato or *maschile*. The word used here could be helpful if the gender is not apparent from the baby's name. The baby was born of Vittoria Veloce, "his legitimate wife," and the informant, so now we know that the informant is also the father of the baby.

Section D provides information about the father of the baby. In this example everything is listed as *come sopra* ("same as above"), meaning that the father is the informant and his information is stated above. If the informant were not the father, you would see the name, age, occupation and residence of the father here.

Section E lists the actual date, time and place of the baby's birth. Remember that this date could be several days prior to the date of this document's registration, shown at the top of the page. In this example the baby was born April 10, and her birth was registered April 11.

Page two of this birth record continues in Figures 8-4, 8-5 and 8-6. It starts off with the name of the baby, Maria.

The next section of the document (F) gives information about the two witnesses. Pay attention to these names because sometimes you will find other relatives acting as witnesses. In this example, both witnesses are named Stramaglia and the phrase *cugino del dichiarante* indicates that they are cousins of the informant.

The last paragraph formalizes the record. If the informant or witnesses were literate, they would have signed their names; in this example they were not.

The free formatted paragraph at the bottom of the document (G) is an example of a margin notation. The original document was recorded in 1847, the margin notation in 1868, some 21 years later. It provides information about the baby's marriage. It not only states when, where and who she married, it even provides the document number. If we already knew her husband's name, this notation confirms that we have found the correct birth record. If we did not yet have her marriage information, we now know where to find it. It is very important to always translate any margin notations you find.

Figure 8-7 shows how to use a Data Extract Form

for this birth record. The important genealogical information from the original document is copied to the Data Extract Form. Blank Data Extract Forms are in Appendix D, along with a detailed discussion about how to use them.

Now that you have had an overview of a typical *atto di nascita*, try to read the first format of this document on your own. Use the word lists in Appendix A to help you. If you get stuck deciphering the handwriting, first try using the handwriting tips presented in the last chapter, then use the second format of the document. If you have problems in translation, use format three to assist you. There is another *atto di nascita* in chapter ten that you may use for practice. Since the civil vital records are so consistent, after reviewing just a few birth records, you should be able to read any birth record you might find.

Marriage Records

The Italian *Stato Civile* include several different types of marriage records. The betrothed couple had to publish their marriage banns, called *notificazioni* or *pubblicazioni*, usually a few weeks to a few months before the wedding. This document stated their intention to marry and gave the public a chance to oppose their union. If the bride and groom were born in different towns, the *notificazione* was created in both towns. Its purpose was to prevent a person from having two spouses or from marrying a cousin (although cousins could receive special dispensation from the church).

The marriage banns had to be posted on the door of the church or the city hall for at least two consecutive Sundays (sometimes three Sundays or two Sundays plus a Thursday) and were also read aloud in church or in the main square on those days because most people were illiterate.

Another set of marriage documents, called *processetti* or *allegati*, contains all the documentation the couple provided in order to marry. This included the birth records of both the bride and the groom, the permission of their parents (or if the parents were dead, their death records), the marriage banns (and proof showing no opposition to their union), and death records of previous spouses (if either had been married before). It wasn't easy to get married in nineteenth-century Italy!

You can see how valuable this set of documents could be to your genealogical research. You get many documents for the price of one. Unfortunately, the *processetti* are not as common as the other documents. If they are available for your town and time period, seek them out. If not, the other marriage documents provide the information you need.

The marriage record may be one of two kinds. The *Atto di Solenne Promessa di Matrimonio* is the record of the solemn promise to marry. It was usually recorded shortly before the wedding took place. The *Atto di Matrimonio* is the record of the marriage. You will usually find either one or the other. The clerks sometimes used the forms indiscriminately, so you may find an *Atto di Solenne Promessa di Matrimonio* recorded after the actual wedding ceremony occurred. Both types of documents contain identical information, so for purposes of this discussion we will use the term marriage record for either one.

Of all three types of marriage documents, it is easiest to find the marriage record because it was recorded the closest in time to the actual marriage ceremony. If there are *processetti* available, seek them out next. The *notificazione*, which contains the same information as the marriage record, is generally not worth seeking, unless you are unable to find any other marriage documents.

Let's look at some actual examples of Italian *Stato Civile* marriage documents.

Pubblicazioni or *Notificazioni*—Wedding Banns

The first document that an engaged couple recorded at the town hall was the wedding banns, called *pubblicazioni* or *notificazioni* in Italian. This document had to be recorded in the town of birth of both the bride and groom. If they were born in different towns, you will find two copies, one recorded in each town. The *pubblicazioni* contain the date, time and place of its creation, as well as the name and title of the official recording it (usually the mayor in small towns). This recording process usually took place at least several weeks before the

planned marriage. The document also provides the names, ages, occupations, birthplaces and residences of the betrothed, as well as similar information about their parents. Two witnesses and their information were also included.

As the banns were read aloud to the public and posted on the appropriate days, the clerk recorded these facts on the document and signed it, proving that the correct process was followed.

Figures 8-8, 8-9 and 8-10 show a typical *pubblicazioni di matrimonio* for Pietro Moffa and Maria Lalli in three different formats. The first format is the original document. The second format replaces the handwritten Italian script with typed Italian script, to assist in deciphering the handwriting. The third format replaces the Italian with English, showing how the document translates. Refer to the second and third formats for the remainder of this discussion.

The first section (A) of all wedding banns, and all records of the *Stato Civile*, consists of the same information. It states the date and time that the registration occurred. Note that the numbers used in the date are written out as words. This section also names the recording official and his title.

The next section (B) gives the valuable genealogical information about the future bride and groom. In this document the last names are presented first, for example, Moffa Pietro Antonio. The only way to tell if the names are written last name first (as on this document) or first name first (as in other documents we will review) is by familiarity with Italian names. Appendix A (Italian Word Lists) includes a list of common Italian first names to help you with this.

Section C contains the legal boilerplate stating that there are no obstacles to this union, as confirmed by the two witnesses.

The last section (D) mostly handwritten, discusses the documentation provided by the couple (their birth records) and the presence of the groom's parents, who give their consent to the marriage. An interesting document mentioned here is the military discharge papers presented by the groom. The date and place of their issuance is provided, making it easy to obtain this document, if desired.

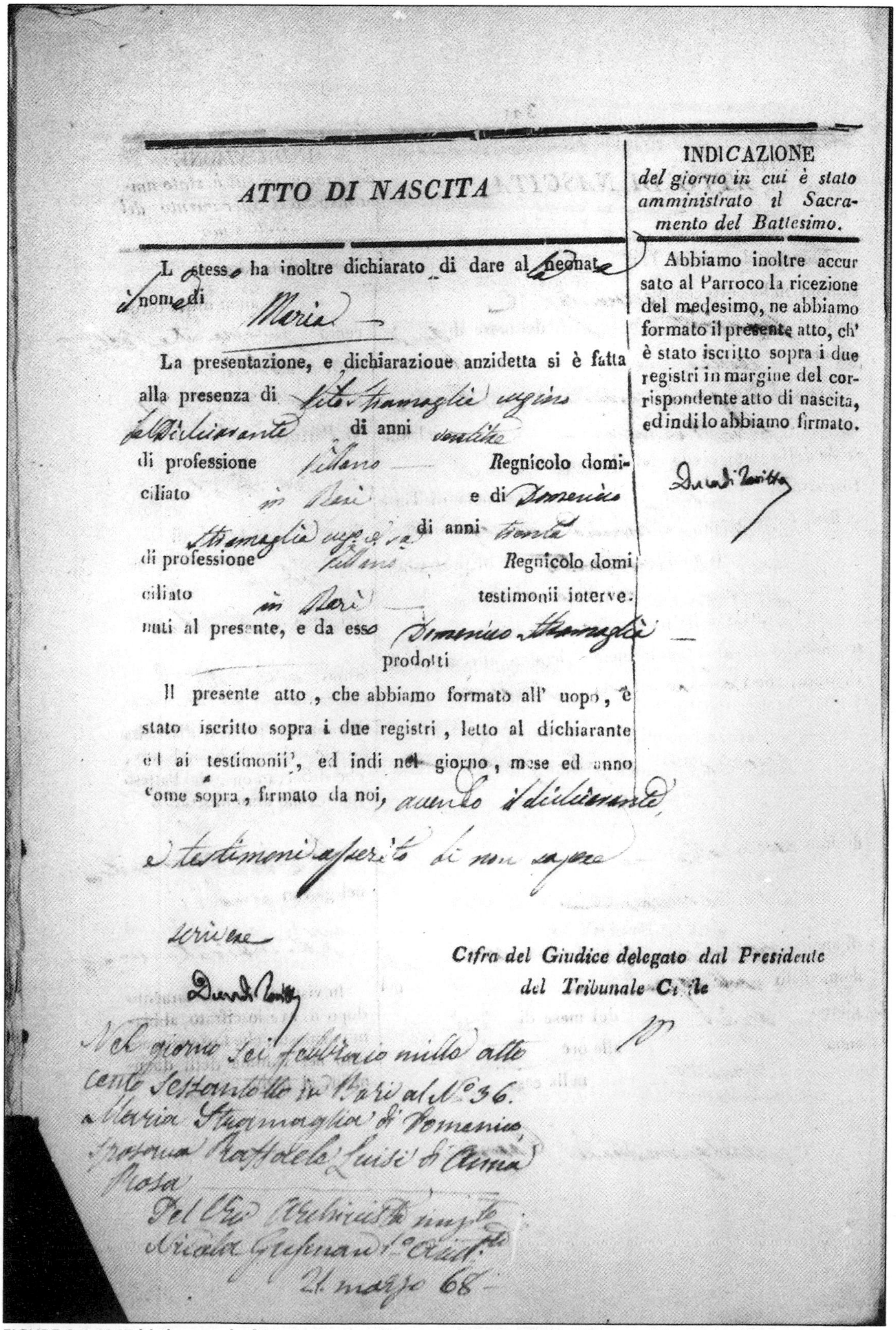

ATTO DI NASCITA

L' *stesso* ha inoltre dichiarato di dare al *neonat* nome di

Maria

La presentazione, e dichiarazioue anzidetta si è fatta alla presenza di *Sito Stramaglia uigiro*

il dichiarante di anni *ventitre*

di professione *villano* Regnicolo domiciliato *in Bari* e di *Domenico*

Stramaglia uigio sra di anni *trenta*

di professione *villano* Regnicolo domiciliato *in Bari* testimonii intervenuti al presente, e da esso *Domenico Stramaglia* prodotti

Il presente atto, che abbiamo formato all' uopo, è stato iscritto sopra i due registri, letto al dichiarante et ai testimonii, ed indi nel giorno, mese ed anno come sopra, firmato da noi, *avendo il dichiarante*

e testimoni asserito di non sapere

scrivere

Duca di Zovitta

Cifra del Giudice delegato dal Presidente del Tribunale Civile

Abbiamo inoltre accusato al Parroco la ricezione del medesimo, ne abbiamo formato il presente atto, ch' è stato iscritto sopra i due registri in margine del corrispondente atto di nascita, ed indi lo abbiamo firmato.

Duca di Zovitta

FIGURE 8-4 **1847 birth record of Maria Stramaglia, second page, original format. (Photograph courtesy of the Family History Library of The Church of Jesus Christ of Latter-day Saints)**

ATTO DI NASCITA

	INDICAZIONE del giorno in cui è stato amministrato il Sacramento del Battesimo.

Lo stesso ha inoltre dichiarato di dare alla neonata il nome di *Maria*

La presentazione, e dichiarazioue anzidetta si è fatta alla presenza di *Vito Stramaglia cugino del Dichiarante* **di anni** *ventitre* di professione *villano* *Regnicolo* domiciliato in *Bari* e di *Domenico Stramaglia cugino* **di anni** *trenta* di professione *villano* *Regnicolo* domiciliato in *Bari* testimonii interve. nuti al presente, e da esso *Domenico Stramaglia* prodotti

Il presente atto, che abbiamo formato all' uopo, è stato iscritto sopra i due registri, letto al dichiarante et ai testimonii', e l indi nel giorno, mese ed anno. come sopra, firmato da noi, avendo il dichiarante

e testimoni asserito di non sapere

scrivere

David Toritto

Abbiamo inoltre accursato al Parroco la ricezione del medesimo, ne abbiamo formato il presente atto, ch' è stato iscritto sopra i due registri in margine del corrispondente atto di nascita, ed indi lo abbiamo firmato.

David Toritto

Cifra del Giudice delegato dal Presidente del Tribunale Civile

Nel giorno sei febbraio mille otto cento sessantotto in Bari al N.º 36 Maria Stramaglia di Domenico sposara Raffaele Luisi di Anna Rosa

FIGURE 8-5 **1847 birth record of Maria Stramaglia, second page, transcribed format.**

BIRTH ACT

The same has also declared to give to the infant

the name of *Maria*

The aforesaid presentation and declaration was made

in the presence of *Vito Stramaglia cousin*
of the informant age *twenty three*
occupation *peasant* citizen residing *in Bari* and of *Domenico*
Stramaglia cousin age *thirty*
occupation *peasant* citizen residing *in Bari* witnesses taking
part at present, and of himself *Domenico Stramaglia*
produced

The present act, that we have created as necessary, and
was written above as two copies, read to the informant
and to the witnesses, and then on the day, month and year
above, signed by us, *the informant and the*
witnesses have asserted they do not know how
to write

David Joritto

Signature of the delegated Judge of the President
of the Civil Court

NOTICE
of the day on which was
administered the Sacra-
ment of Baptism

We have also acknowledg-
ed to the Rector the receipt
of the same, we have
created the present act which
was written above in the two
registers in the margins of the
corresponding birth act,
and that we have signed.

David Joritto

On day six February one thousand eight
hundred sixty eight in Bari at number 36
Maria Stramaglia (dau) of Domenico
married Raffaele Luisi (son) of Anna
Rosa

FIGURE 8-6 **1847 birth record of Maria Stramaglia, second page, translated format.**

Data Extract Form

Stato Civile of Italy—Birth Record of: **Maria Stramaglia**

Document Source

Microfilm: **1518156**	Title: **Stato Civile, Bari, Nati, 1846-1849**
Year: **1847**	Document Number: **321**

Record Creation

Date: **11 April 1847 16:00**

Clerk: **Francesco Saverio Caravita D'Toritto**

Place: **Bari**

Informant

Name: **Domenico Stramaglia**	Age: **ventiquattro (24)**
Birthplace:	Son/Dau of:
Occupation: **villano**	Residence: **Bari**

Parents

	Mother	Father
Name:	Vittoria Veloce	Domenico Stramaglia
Birthplace:		
Age:	ventiquattro (24)	ventiquattro (24)
Dau/Son of:		
Occupation:		villano
Residence:		Bari
Notes:		

Child

Name: **Maria Stramaglia**	Sex: **F**
Birthdate: **10 April 1847 10:00**	Birthplace: **strada Carmine**
Baptism Info: **12 April 1847, parroco della Cattedrale**	
Notes:	

Witnesses

	Witness 1	Witness 2
Name:	Vito Stramaglia (cugino)	Domenico Stramaglia (cugino)
Birthplace:		
Age:	ventitre (23)	trenta (30)
Son/Dau of:		
Occupation:	villano	villano
Residence:	Bari	Bari

Margin Notations

Nel giorno sei febbraio mille otto cento sessantotto in Bari al N°. 36 Maria

Stramaglia di Domenico sposara Raffaele Luisi di Anna Rosa

Miscellaneous Notes

Researcher: **Lynn Nelson**　　　　Date: **June 15, 1994**

FIGURE 8-7 Completed Data Extract Form for the 1847 birth record of Maria Stramaglia.

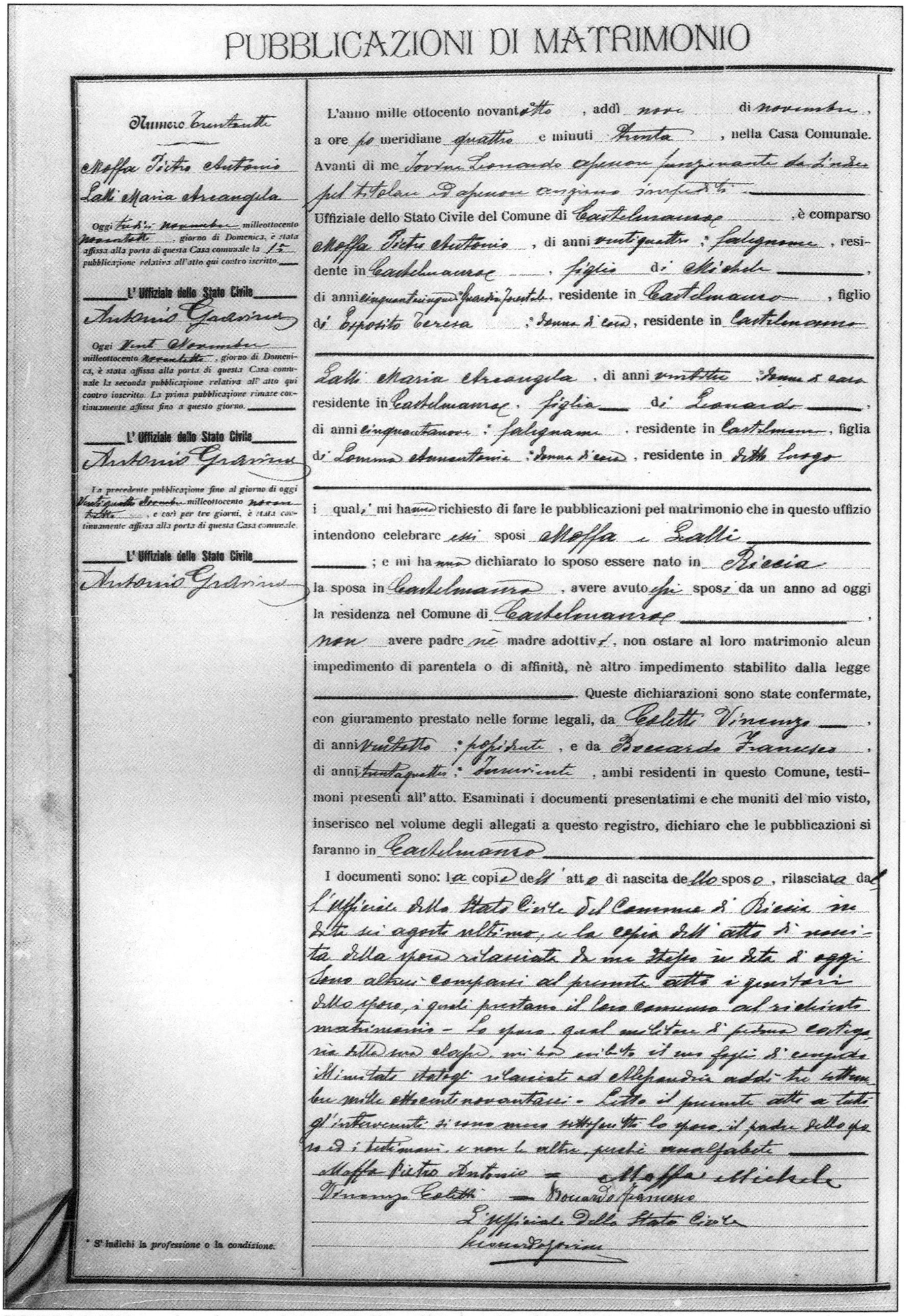

FIGURE 8-8 **1898 marriage banns of Pietro Moffa and Maria Lalli, original format. (Photograph courtesy of the Family History Library of The Church of Jesus Christ of Latter-day Saints)**

PUBBLICAZIONI DI MATRIMONIO

Numero Trentasette

Moffa Pietro Antonio
Lalli Maria Arcangela

Oggi tredici novembre *milleottocento* novantotto *giorno di Domenica, è stata fissa alla porta di questa Casa comunale la pubblicazione relativa all'atto qui contro iscritto.*

L' Uffiziale dello Stato Civile

Antonio Gravina

Oggi venti novembre *milleottocento* novantotto *giorno di Domenica, è stata affissa alla porta di questa Casa comunale la seconda pubblicazione relativa all'atto qui contro iscritto. La prima pubblicazione rimase continuamente affissa fino a questo giorno.*

L' Uffiziale dello Stato Civile

Antonio Gravina

La precedente pubblicazione fino al giorno di oggi ventiquattro novembre milleottocento novantotto, e cosí per tre giorni, è stata continuamente affissa alla porta di questa Casa comunale

L' Uffiziale dello Stato Civile

Antonio Gravina

* *Si indichi la professione o la condizione.*

L'anno mille ottocento novantotto , addì nove di novembre . a ore po meridiane quattro e minuti trenta , nella Casa Comunale. Avanti di me Sovini Leonardo operore funzinante da L'udi- pel titolare ed operore anziano sussedito —————

Uffiziale dello Stato Civile del Comune di Castelmauro , è comparso Moffa Pietro Antonio , di anni ventiquattro , falegname , resi- dente in Castelmauro , figlio di Michele ————— di anni cinquantacinque Guardia Forestale residente in Castelmauro , figlio di Esposito Teresa ,•donna di casa , residente in Castelmauro

Lalli Maria Arcangela , di anni ventitre ,•donna di casa residente in Castelmauro , figlia di Leonardo . di anni cinquantanove ,• falegname , residente in Castelmauro , figlia di Lomma Annantonia ,•donna di casa residente in detto luogo

i quali mi hanno richiesto di fare le pubblicazioni pel matrimonio che in questo uffizio intendono celebrare essi sposi Moffa e Lalli ————— ; e mi hanno dichiarato lo sposo essere nato in Riccia la sposa in Castelmauro . avere avuto essi sposi da un anno ad oggi la residenza nel Comune di Castelmauro ————— non avere padre ne madre adottivo , non ostare al loro matrimonio alcun impedimento di parentela o di affinità, nè altro impedimento stabilito dalla legge ————————————— Queste dichiarazioni sono state confermate, con giuramento prestato nelle forme legali, da Colleti Vincenzo ———, di anni ventiotto ,•possidente , e da Boccardo Francesco , di anni trentaquattro .• Inserviente , ambi residenti in questo Comune, testi- moni presenti all'atto. Esaminati i documenti presentatimi e che muniti del mio visto, inserisco nel volume degli allegati a questo registro, dichiaro che le pubblicazioni si faranno in Castelmauro

I documenti sono: la copia dell' atto di nascita dello sposo , rilasciata dal L'Ufficiale dello Stato Civile del Comune di Riccia in data sei agosto ultimo, e la copia dell' atto di nasci ta della sposa rilasciata da me stesso in data di oggi. Sono altrui comparsi al presente atto i genitori dello sposo, i quali prestano il loro consenso al richiesto matrimonio — Lo sposo qual militare di perdono catego ria della sua elogia. mi ha exibito il uno foglie di congedo illimitato stato gli rilasciato ad Alessandria addi tre settem bre mille ottocento novantasei. Letto il presente atto a tutti gl'intervenuti di uno meco sottoscritto lo sposo, il padre dello spo so ed i testimoni, e non le altri perche analfabeti —————

Moffa Pietro Antonio — Moffa Michele
Vincenzo Colleti — Boccardo Francesco
L'Ufficiale dello Stato Civile
Leonardo Sovini

FIGURE 8-9 **1898 marriage banns of Pietro Moffa and Maria Lalli, transcribed format.**

MARRIAGE BANNS

Number Thirty seven

Moffa Pietro Antonio
Lalli Maria Arcangela

Today thirteen November one thousand eight hundred ninety eight the day of Sunday was affixed to the door of this Town Hall the 15 publication related to the act herewritten

—— The Officer of the Vital Records ——

Antonio Gravina

Today twenty November one thousand eight hundred ninety eight the day of Sunday was affixed to the door of this Town Hall the second publication related to the act herewritten. The first publication remained continuously affixed up to this day.

—— The Officer of the Vital Records ——

Antonio Gravina

The preceding publication up to the day of today twenty four November one thousand eight hundred ninely eight and thus for three days, was continuously affixed to the door of the Town Hall.

—— The Officer of the Vital Records ——

Antonio Gravina

* indicates the profession or occupation

The year one thousand eight hundred ninety eight , the ninth of November at the hour of four post meridian and thirty minutes, in the Town Hall Before me Sovini Leonardo operating functionary of the titled magistrate and operating senior successor Officer of the Vital Records of the Town of Castelmauro , appeared Moffa Pietro Antonio , age ventiquattro ,* falegname , resident of Castelmauro son of Michele , age fifty five *forester resident of Castelmauro , son of Esposito Teresa ;*housewife , resident of Castelmauro

Lalli Maria Arcangela , age twenty three ; housewife resident of Castelmauro , daughter of Leonardo age fifty nine ;*carpenter , resident of Castelmauro daughter of Lomma Annantonia ;* housewife , resident of same place

They have requested me to make the pubblication of marriage in this office which they intend to celebrate, these newlyweds Moffa and Lalli ; and they have declared that the groom was born in Riccia the bride in Castelmauro . the newlyweds have lived from one year to today in residence in the town of Castelmauro they do not have an adoptive father nor an adoptive mother, there are not any impediments of relationship or affinity obstructing their marriage, nor any other impediment according to the law. These declarations are verified, by taking an oath in the legal form, from li, da Colleti Vincenzo age twenty eight ;*property owner and from Boccardo Francesco age trentaquattro .*attendant , both residing in this Town, witnesses present at the act. I examined the documents presented to me and provided my approval, inserted in the volume of annexed records to this register, declaring that the publication would be made in Castelmauro

The documents are: the copy of the birth record of the groom issued by The officer of the Vital Records of the town of Riccia dated last August sixth, and a copy of the birth record of the bride issued by myself today. Others appearing at the present act are the parents of the groom, who give their consent to the requested marriage. — The groom, whose military status of pardoned with honors, has exhibited to me the discharge paper that was issued in Alessandria on the third September one thousand eight hundred ninety six. I read the present act to all the participants with me undersigned the groom, the father of the groom and the witnesses, and not the others because they are illiterate

Moffa Pietro Antonio
Vincenzo Colleti

Moffa Michele
Boccardo Francesco

The Officer of the Vital Records

Leonardo Sovini

FIGURE 8-10 **1898 marriage banns of Pietro Moffa and Maria Lalli, translated format.**

Finally, all parties capable of writing signed their names, in this case, the groom, his father and the two witnesses.

The column on the left side of the page was filled out by the clerk in the weeks that followed the original recording of the document on November 9, 1898. Each time the banns were read aloud and posted, the clerk recorded the date and signed it. In this example the banns were publicized on Sunday, November 13; Sunday, November 20; and Thursday, November 24.

Now that you have had an overview of a typical *pubblicazioni* record, try to read the first format of this document on your own. Use the word lists in Appendix A to help you. After reviewing just a few wedding banns from the *Stato Civile*, you should be able to read any *pubblicazioni* or *notificazioni* you may find.

Atto di Matrimonio—Marriage Record

The actual wedding ceremony always took place in the church, but civil authorities required the civil marriage to be registered at the *casa comunale* (town hall). Sometimes this registration occurred shortly before the wedding, in which case the document will be the *atto di solenne promessa di matrimonio* (the promise to marry). Sometimes it was registered shortly after the wedding, in which case the document will be the *atto di matrimonio*. In some cases, the clerk just used whatever form was available and its title has nothing to do with when it was recorded. In either case, the information included in both of these documents is essentially the same, so we will discuss them together.

Recording the marriage required the presence of not only the bride and groom, but their parents and four witnesses. The bride and groom had to present all appropriate documentation (the *processetti*) at this time. If you're lucky, the clerk would place all of these documents in the marriage book and they may all be filmed together, though usually the *processetti* were stored separately from the marriage record.

The clerk recorded the date, time and place of the registration and the date of the marriage ceremony. The names, ages, occupations, residences and birthplaces of both the bride and groom are included, as well as the names, occupations and residences of both sets of parents. The names, ages, occupations and residences of the four witnesses were also recorded. If any of the parties were able to write, they would sign the document.

Figures 8-11, 8-12 and 8-13 show the first page of the marriage record in the three different formats that we have been using throughout this chapter. The first format is the original document. The second format replaces the handwritten Italian script with typed Italian script. The third format replaces the Italian with English. For the rest of this discussion, use the second and third formats for reference.

Figure 8-12, the marriage record of Domenico Quartodipalo and Arcangela Savino, is a typical example of an *atto di solenne promessa di matrimonio*. Notice how the page is divided into two sections. The civil information is recorded in the body of the document (the left side) while the church information is recorded in the right column.

As previously discussed, the first section (A) is the same in all records of the *Stato Civile* and hence, all marriage records. It states the date and time that the registration occurred. Note that the numbers used in the date are written out as words and the use of the 24-hour clock (*ventitre*, 23 hours is 11:00 P.M.). In the original format (Figure 8-11) the first written word, *sessantaquattro* (sixty-four) contains good examples of the typical lowercase *s* of that time. If you were ignorant to the nineteenth-century style of handwriting, you might easily mistake these variations of the lowercase *s* for *f*s. The name and title of the official who recorded the marriage and location (town, district and province) is always included in this section.

Note that the date written in section A is the date that the promise to marry was recorded, not necessarily the date of the marriage ceremony. The date of the actual marriage is found in the right margin with the church information. In this case, both occurred on February 20, 1864. It appears that the promise was actually recorded after the ceremony because this document was created at 11:00 P.M..

Section B presents the groom's information. In the name, D. Domenico Quartodipalo, the upper-

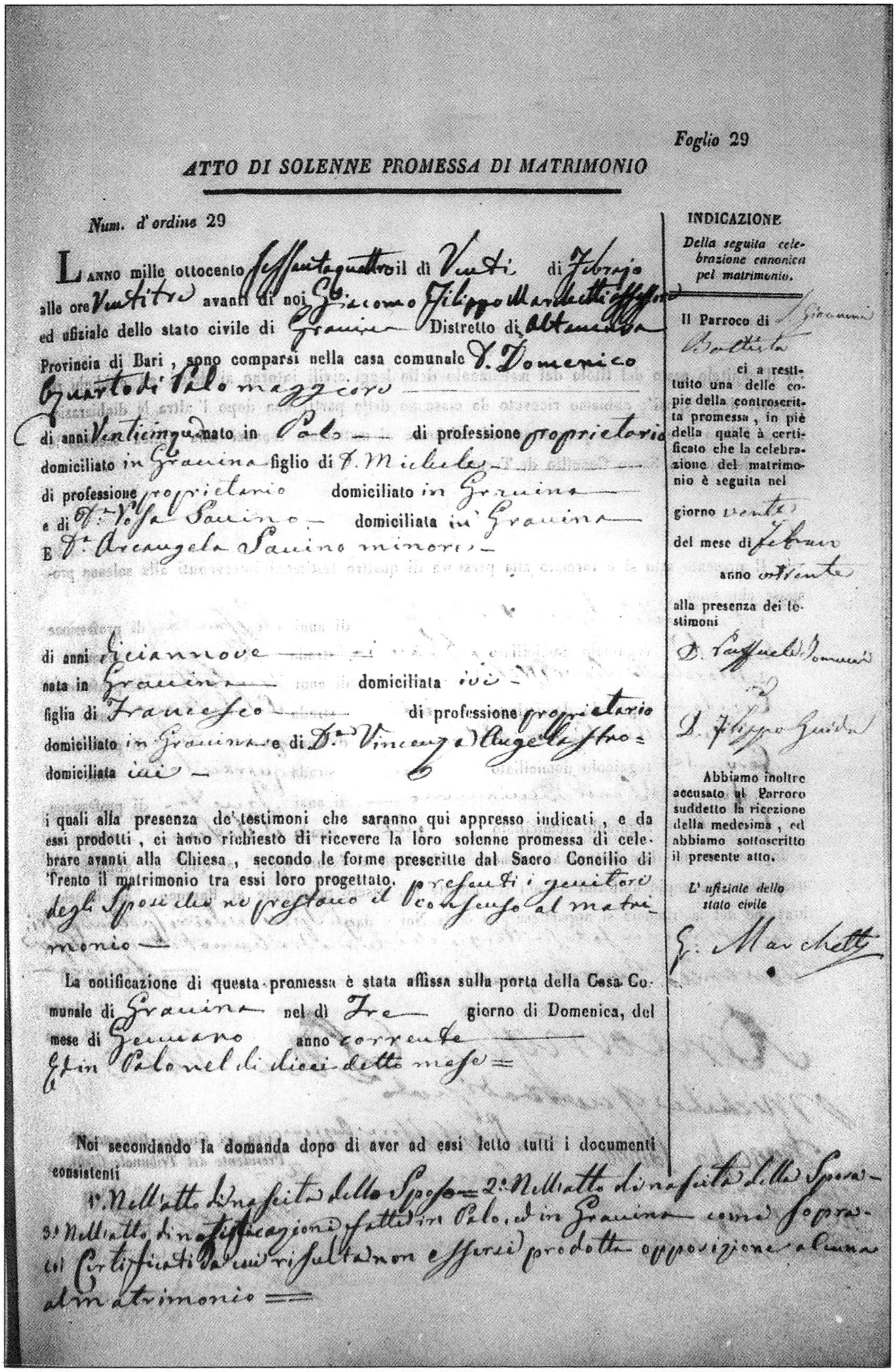

FIGURE 8-11 **1864 marriage record of Domenico Quartodipalo and Arcangela Savino, first page, original format. (Photograph courtesy of the Family History Library of The Church of Jesus Christ of Latter-day Saints)**

ATTO DI SOLENNE PROMESSA DI MATRIMONIO

Num. d'ordine 29

L'ANNO mille ottocento sessantaquattro il dì venti di febraio alle ore ventitre avanti di noi Giacomo Filippo Marchetti assessore ed ufficiale dello stato civile di Gravina Distretto di Altamura Provincia di Bari, sono comparsi nella casa comunale D. Domenico QuartodiPalo maggiore

di anni venticinque nato in Palo di professione proprietario domiciliato in Gravina figlio di D. Michele di professione proprietario domiciliato in Gravina e di D.ª Rosa Savino domiciliata in Gravina

E D.ª Arcangela Savino minore

di anni diciannove nata in Gravina domiciliata ivi figlia di Francesco di professione proprietario domiciliato in Gravina e di D.ª Vincenza Angelastro domiciliata ivi

i quali alla presenza de' testimoni che saranno qui appresso indicati, e da essi prodotti, ci anno richiesto di ricevere la loro solenne promessa di celebrare avanti alla Chiesa, secondo le forme prescritte dal Sacro Concilio di Trento il matrimonio tra essi loro progettato presenti i genitori degli sposi che ne prestano il consenso al matri— monio

La notificazione di questa promessa è stata affissa sulla porta della Casa Comunale di Gravina nel dì Tre giorno di Domenica, del mese di gennaro anno corrente Ed in Palo nel di dieci dello mese

Noi secondando la domanda dopo di aver ad essi letto tutti i documenti consistenti 1º. Nell'atto di nascita dello Sposo = 2º. Nell'atto di nascita della Sposa — 3º. Nell'atti di notificazioni fatto in Palo, ed in Gravina come sopra — 4º. Certificati da essi risulta non essersi prodotta opposizione alcuna al matrimonio

---

INDICAZIONE

Della seguita celebrazione canonica pel matrimonio.

Il Parroco di S. Giovanni Battista ci a restituito una delle copie della controscritta promessa, in piè della quale à certificato che la celebrazione del matrimonio è seguita nel

giorno venti

del mese di febraio

anno corrente

alla presenza dei testimoni

D. Raffaele Tomaci

D. Filippo Guida

Abbiamo inoltre accusato al Parroco suddetto la ricezione della medesima, ed abbiamo sottoscritto il presente atto.

L' uffziale dello stato civile

G. Marchetti

FIGURE 8-12 **1864 marriage record of Domenico Quartodipalo and Arcangela Savino, first page, transcribed format.**

ACT OF THE SOLEMN PROMISE OF MATRIMONY

Ordinal No. 29

In the year one thousand eight hundred *sixty four* day *twenty* of *February* at the hour of *twenty three* before us *Giacomo Filippo Marchetti councilman* and officers of the Vital Records of *Gravina* District of *Altamura* Province of Bari , appeared in the town hall *D. Domenico*

QuartodiPalo of legal age

age *twenty five* born in *Palo* occupation *property owner* living *in Gravina* son of *D. Michele* occupation *property owner* living *in Gravina* and of *Dª Rosa Savino* living *in Gravina*

and *Dª Arcangela Savino minor*

age *nineteen* born in *Gravina* living *there* daughter of *Francesco* occupation *property owner* living *in Gravina* and of *Dª Vincenza Angelastro* living *there*

whom in the presence of witnesses that will be indicated next, and give these results, have requested us to receive their solemn promise to celebrate in the Church, according to the form prescribed by the Sacred Council of Trent the planned marriage between them. *in attendance are the parents of the spouses that give them their consent to marry*

The notification of this promise was affixed on the door of the Town Hall of *Gravina* on day *three* a Sunday in the month of *January* year *current* *and in Palo on the tenth of the month*

We are seconding their application after having read to them all of the documents consisting:

1ˢᵗ Of the birth act of the groom = 2ⁿᵈ Of the birth act of the bride 3ʳᵈ Of the banns made in Palo, and in Gravina as above — 4ᵗʰ Of the certificates of these proving there was no opposition to the marriage

NOTICE

Of the following celebration of the canonical marriage

The rector of *S. Giovanni Battista* has returned to us a copy of the here-written promise, at the bottom of which he has certified that the celebration of the marriage occurred on

day *twenty* of the month of *February* year *current*

in the presence of the witnesses

D. Raffaele Tomaci

D. Filippo Guida

We have also acknowledged to the rector above the receipt of the same, and we have undersigned the present act.

The officer of the vital records

G. Marchetti

FIGURE 8-13 1864 marriage record of Domenico Quartodipalo and Arcangela Savino, first page, translated format.

case *D* is the abbreviation for *Don*, a title of respect. His mother's name, Dᵃ. Rosa Savino, uses the female version, *Dònna*.

Section C includes the bride's information. The word *minore*, following the bride's name, and the word *maggiore*, following the groom's name, indicate their legal status. The bride is a minor (under twenty-one) and requires her parents' consent to marry. The groom is twenty-five, past the age of majority.

Section D includes the typical legal boilerplate which states that the couple will be married in the church according to the Sacred Council of Trent. It also mentions the presence of the parents and their consent to the marriage.

The next section (E) covers the status of the *notificazioni*, stating when and where they were posted. Since the bride and groom were born in different towns, the *notificazioni* were posted in both towns.

Section F lists all the documents of the *processetti* that the couple presented in order to be married.

Page two of this marriage record is continued in Figures 8-14, 8-15 and 8-16. Section G provides the information about the four witnesses. Take note of these people because they may be friends, neighbors or relatives, and this information may later help you with your research. Notice how, for each witness, the last name is written before the first name. You will see both methods of listing names throughout the *Stato Civile*. In this case it is obvious which is the first name and which is the last name because the word *Signor* clarifies it. Familiarity with Italian names also is helpful in making this distinction.

The occupation of the third witness is listed as *servente*. This is an example of an ambiguous Italian word that is open to interpretation. One dictionary provides three different meanings. An obsolete definition is a servant. Since this document was written in 1864, this is a possibility. However, the bride and groom, their families and all the other witnesses appear to be rather well-to-do (middle-class property owners), so it is unlikely that a servant would be included in this group, especially since his name is qualified with *Signor*, a term of respect.

Another definition of *servente* is a gunner, a person who uses or is in charge of ordnance. Looking up the word gunner in the English side of the dictionary shows both *servente* and *artigliere* (artilleryman) as definitions. This document was written in the middle of the reunification of Italy, a time of much political debate and fighting, so this could be an appropriate occupation for this time period. However, the witness with this occupation is forty-eight years old, a bit old for a soldier.

The third definition of *servente* is as an adjective meaning, *in waiting*, as in a gentleman in waiting. Since this is an adjective, it is unlikely it would be used as a noun for an occupation. In analyzing these three possibilities, you can only use logic and the process of elimination to help decide which definition is most likely.

The last part of the document (H) includes the signature of not only the officer of the vital records, but the bride and groom, their fathers, and the witnesses, since they are all able to write (although not too well, in the case of the bride, who even spelled her name wrong). Note that the paragraph above the signatures mentions that the mothers are not able to write.

Figure 8-17 shows the Data Extract Form for this marriage record. The important genealogical information from the original document is copied to the Data Extract Form. Blank Data Extract Forms are in Appendix D, along with a detailed discussion about how to use them.

The marriage record is an important document for genealogical research, since it provides a lot of information. For example, the birthplaces and ages of the bride and groom give us enough information to pursue their birth records. It also indicates, in this example, that the parents of the couple are still alive, which helps narrow down their dates of death for seeking out their death records.

Now that you have had an overview of a typical marriage record, try to read the first format of this document on your own. Use the word lists in Appendix A to help you. If you have problems in translation, use format three. There is another marriage record in chapter ten that you also may use for practice.

ed il capitolo sesto del titolo del matrimonio delle leggi civili intorno ai dritti ed obblighi rispettivi degli sposi; abbiamo ricevuto da ciascuno delle parti, una dopo l'altra le dichiarazioni ch' Elleno solennemente promettono di celebrare il matrimoni innanzi alla Chiea secondo le
forme dettate dal Sacro Concilio di Trento.

Il presente atto si è formato alla presenza di quattro testimoni intervenuti alla solenne promessa che sono

1. _Caporelli_ Signor _Michele_ — di anni _Sessanta_ di professione
Civile regnicolo domiciliato _Gravina_ strada _Borgo_ — num.

2. _Marchetti_ Signor _Ercole_ — di anni _Trentotto_ di professione
Civile regnicolo domiciliato _ivi_ strada _S. Sebastiano_ num.

3. _Giannelli_ Signor _Pietro_ — di anni _quarantotto_ di professione
Servente regnicolo domiciliato _ivi_ strada _quarantotto_ num.

4. _Linuelli_ Signor _Beniamino_ — di anni _Trenta_ di professione
Civile regnicolo domiciliato _ivi_ strada _S. Sofia_ num.

e dopo di averne dato lettura a' testimoni suddetti ed ai futuri sposi, ai quali ne abbiamo altresì date due copie uniformi da noi sottoscritte per essere presentate al Parroco, cui la celebrazione del matrimonio si appartiene, si è da Noi e dagli Sposi, e dei rispettivi padri,
e dai Testimonii sottoscritto, giacchè le madre hanno detto non sapere
scrivere —

Domenico Quartodipalo —

Arcangla Savino

Michele Quartodipalo

Francesco Savino

Giacomo Marchetti

L'assessore Anziano Cifra del Giudice Delegato, dal
Presidente del Tribunale Civile

Testimonii
Michele Caporelli

Ercole Marchetti

FIGURE 8-14 **1864 marriage record of Domenico Quartodipalo and Arcangela Savino, second page, original format. (Photograph courtesy of the Family History Library of The Church of Jesus Christ of Latter-day Saints)** ed il capitolo sesto del titolo del matrimonio delle leggi civili intorno ai dritti ed obblighi rispettivi degli sposi ; abbiamo ricevuto da ciascuno delle parti, una dopo l' altra le dichiarazioni ch' Elleno solennemente promettose di celebrare il matrimoni innanzi alla Chiesa secondo le forme dettate dal Sacro Concilio di Trento.

Il presente atto si è formato alla presenza di quattro testimoni intervenuti alla solenne promessa che sono

1. Caporelli Signor Michele Civile regnicolo domiciliato a Gravina di anni Sessanta di professione strada Borgo num.
2. Marchetti Signor Ercole Civile regnicolo domiciliato ivi di anni Trentotto di professione strada S. Sebastiano num.
3. Giannelli Signor Pietro Servente regnicolo domiciliato ivi di anni quarantotto di professione strada quarantotto num.
4. Linulpi Signor Beniamino Civile regnicolo domiciliato ivi di anni Trenta di professione strada S. Sofia num.

e dopo di averne dato lettura a' testimoni suddetti ed ai futuri sposi, ai quali ne abbiamo altresì data due copie uniformi da noi sottoscritte per essere presentate al Parroco , cui la celebrazione del matrimonio si appartiene , si è, da Noi, e dagli Sposi, e dei rispettini padri e dei Testimonii sotto scritto giacche lei madri hanno detto non sapere = scrivere

Domenico Quartodipalo

Arcangla Savino

Michele Quartodipalo

Francesco Savino = L'assessore Cifra del Giudice Delegato dal Presidente del Tribunale Civile

Testimonii Giacomo Marchetti

Michele Caporelli

Ercole Marchetti

FIGURE 8-15 **1864** marriage record of Domenico Quartodipalo and Arcangela Savino, second page, transcribed format.

and chapter six of the civil marriage laws about the respective rights and obligations
of the spouses ; we have received from each of the parties, one after the other, the declarations
that they solemnly promise to celebrate the marriage before the Church according to the
format dictated by the Sacred Council of Trent.

The present act was created in the presence of four witnesses participating in the solemn pro-
who are

1. *Caporelli Signor Michele*
   middle class citizen residing   *at Gravina*   age *Sixty*   occupation
      street *Borgo*   no.
2. *Marchetti Signor Ercole*
   middle class citizen residing   *there*   age *Thirty eight*   occupation
      street *S. Sebastiano*   no.
3. *Giannelli Signor Pietro*
   (see text) citizen residing   *there*   age *forty eight*   occupation
      street *forty eight*   no.
4. *Linulpi Signor Beniamino*
   middle class citizen residing   *there*   age *Thirty*   occupation
      street *S. Sofia*   no.

and after having read this to the above witnesses and to the future spouses , to each we have also
given two exact copies from us the undersigned to be presented to the rector , who
will perform the marriage ceremony , it is from Us and of *the spouses, and of the respective fathers
and of the witnesses undersigned since the mothers have stated they don't know how
= to write*

Domenico Quartodipalo

Arcangla   *Savino*

Michele Quartodipalo

Francesco Savino   = *L'assessore*

Testimonii   *Giacomo Marchetti*

Michele Caporelli

Ercole Marchetti

*Signature of the Delegated Judge of the
President of the Civil Court*

FIGURE 8-16 **1864 marriage record of Domenico Quartodipalo and Arcangela Savino, second page, translated format.**

Data Extract Form

Stato Civile of Italy—Marriage Record of: **Domenico Quartodipalo**

and: **Arcangela Savino**

Document Source

Microfilm: **1603621**	Title: **Stato Civile, Gravina Matrimoni 1861-1865**
Year: **1864**	Document Number: **29**

Record Creation

Date: **20 February 1864 23:00**
Clerk: **Giacomo Filippo Marchetti**
Place: **Gravina**

Marriage Date:

	Groom	Bride
Name:	D. Domenico QuartodiPalo	C.ª Arcangela Savino
Birthplace:	Palo	Gravina
Age:	venticinque (25)	diciannove (19)
Occupation:	proprietario	
Residence:	Gravina	Gravina
Notes:	maggiore	minore
Father:	D. Michele	Francesco
Occupation:	proprietario	proprietario
Residence:	Gravina	Gravina
Mother:	D.ª Rosa Savino	D.ª Vincenza Angelastro
Occupation:		
Residence:	Gravina	Gravina

Witnesses

	Witness 1	Witness 2
Name:	Caporelli Signor Michele	Marchetti Signor Ercole
Birthplace:		
Age:	sessanta (60)	trentotto (38)
Son/Dau of:		
Occupation:	civile	civile
Residence:	Gravina strada Borgo	Gravina strada S. Sebastiano

	Witness 3	Witness 4
Name:	Gianelli Signor Pietro	Marchetti Signor Ercole
Birthplace:		
Age:	quarantotto (48)	trenta (30)
Son/Dau of:		
Occupation:	servente	civile
Residence:	Gravina strada 48	Gravina strada S. Sofia

Miscellaneous Notes

Researcher: **Lynn Nelson**   Date: **November 13, 1994**

FIGURE 8-17 **Completed Data Extract Form for the 1864 marriage of Domenico Quartodipalo and Arcangela Savino.**

Processetti

The *processetti* or *allegati* are the documents that the bride and groom had to present to be married. Generally, they consist of their birth records, the death records of their parents (if they are no longer living), the *pubblicazioni* of the wedding banns, and proof that there was no opposition to their union. If both parents and the paternal grandfather of the bride or groom were dead, the death record of the paternal grandfather may also be part of the *processetti*. If either the bride or groom had been married before, the death record of the late spouse would also be included.

These documents that the bride and groom presented were really extracts of the originals. The clerks would use special forms to extract the information from the original book. These extracts are almost identical to the original documents, so we will not review any examples of *processetti* documents. A birth extract looks just like a birth record, a *pubblicazioni* extract looks just like the original *pubblicazioni*, and a death record extract looks just like the original death record.

If *processetti* are available for the town and time period of your ancestors, they may be worth seeking. They may be especially important if some of the documents are not otherwise available. For example, if the death record of your ancestor's paternal grandfather precedes the availability of the microfilmed records, you may find an extract of that record in the *processetti*.

Atto di Morte—Death Record

The death record, *atto di morte*, like all records of the *Stato Civile*, was recorded at the *casa comunale*. Two informants, usually friends, neighbors, or sometimes relatives of the deceased would register the death. The recording officer would usually accompany the informants to view the body of the deceased, although sometimes the informants would bring two additional witnesses instead, especially in more recent years and in large cities.

The death record usually includes the date and place that the document was recorded and the name and title of the clerk. The names, ages, occupations and residences of the informants are also

stated. The date and time of the death, along with the deceased's name, age, occupation and residence are listed. Information about the deceased's spouse, father and mother is also usually included. Very rarely will the cause of death be noted. When it is, it is usually something vague, like fever or plague, since medical science was not very advanced at that time.

The death record may be particularly valuable when your ancestor's birth and marriage precede the beginning of the civil records in about 1809. Sometimes it is the only way to determine the parents of an ancestor. It is possible to discover two or even three generations using death records alone. Researching death records of the early nineteenth century allows you to discover ancestors born in the early 1700s, even though the civil records don't begin until 1809.

Figures 8-18, 8-19 and 8-20 show the same death record in the three different formats. Again, the first format is the original document. The second format replaces the handwritten Italian script with typed Italian script and the third format replaces the Italian with English, showing how the document translates. Refer to the second and third formats for this discussion.

Figure 8-19, the death record of Leonarda Catelino, is a typical example of an *atto di morte*. The first section (A) of all records of the *Stato Civile*, including all death records, is the same. It states the date and time that the registration occurred, which is not the date and time of the death. Note that the numbers used in the date are written out as words and the use of the 24-hour clock (*ventuno*, 21 hours, is 9:00 P.M.). The name and title of the official who recorded the death and the location (town, district and province) are also always included in this section.

Section B provides the names, ages, occupations and residences of the two informants. In this example the residence information includes the town and street. Notice that the last name of the second informant, Grumo, is split across two lines. There is a small underscore at the end of the first line, indicating that the word is continued on the next line.

The next section (C) provides the information

about the deceased and his or her death. The date given in this section is the date of death, which is not necessarily the same as the date in section A, which is the date of the recording of this document. The death was often recorded the day after it occurred. In this example the death was recorded on the same day, the ninth of September.

The date, time and place of death, along with the name, birthplace, age, occupation and residence of the deceased are stated. The parents' names, occupations and residence are also shown. Notice in this example that both parents' names are preceded by the word *fu*. This indicates that they are deceased, which can help in tracking down their death records.

The last sentence in this section indicates that the deceased was the widow of *fu Dòn Francesco Savino*. This information is important because it confirms that this is the Leonarda Catelino for whom we are searching because we already knew her husband's name. It also tells us that Francesco Savino died before September 1832, which can assist us in finding his death record.

Section D formalizes the death and includes the signatures of the informants if they were able to write.

Figure 8-21 shows the use of a Data Extract Form for this death record. The important genealogical information from the original document is copied onto the Data Extract Form.

The *Stato Civile* documents that we have covered in this chapter represent typical examples of what you may find for your own ancestors. There are variations, of course, but these samples should provide you with enough familiarity to make you comfortable when you encounter a variation.

Now that you have had an overview of these documents, try to read the first format of each example on your own. Remember to use the word lists in Appendix A to help you. If you get stuck deciphering the handwriting, first try using the handwriting tips presented in the last chapter, then use the second format of the document. If you have problems in translation, try using format three. After reviewing just a few of each type of document, you should be able to read any documents you may find. Chapter ten includes additional records for practice.

You may come across documents that were not created on preprinted forms, but were simply written out by the clerk. In these cases, read them carefully and you will discover that they contain the same words, phrases and information that are on the preprinted documents. They will take a little extra effort to read, but you should have no great problems.

The next chapter shows you how to obtain the records you need.

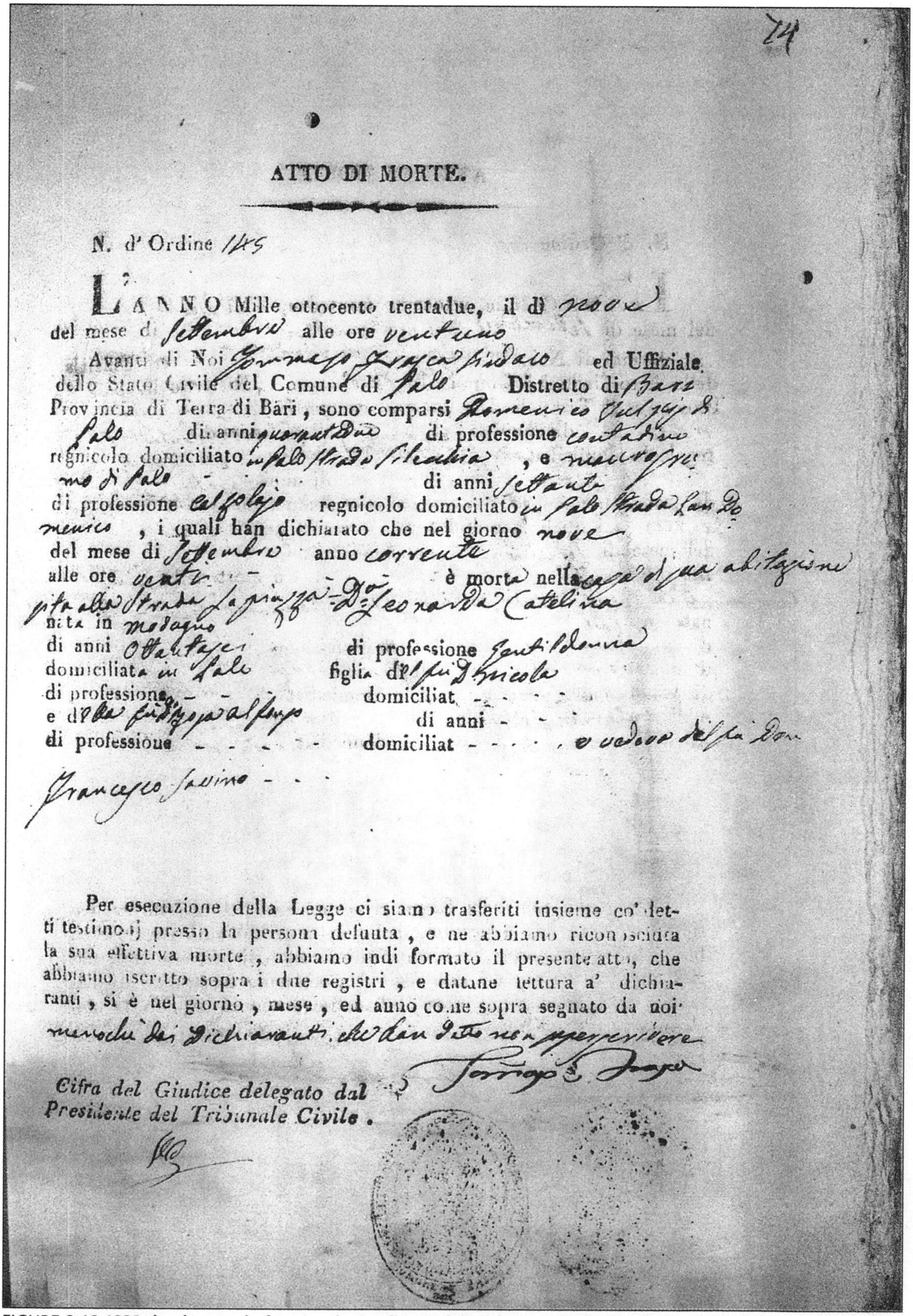

FIGURE 8-18 **1832 death record of Leonarda Catelino, original format. (Photograph courtesy of the Family History Library of The Church of Jesus Christ of Latter-day Saints)**

ATTO DI MORTE.

N. d'Ordine 145

L'ANNO Mille ottocento trentadue, il dì nove del mese d' settembre alle ore ventuno Avanti di Noi Tommaso Frasca Sindaco ed Uffiziale della Stato Civile del Comune di Palo Distretto di Bari Provincia di Terra di Bàri, sono comparsi Domenico Vulgcis di Palo di anni quarantadue di professione contadino regnicolo domiciliato in Palo Strada Silecchia, e Mauro Grumo di Palo di anni settanta di professione calzolaio regnicolo domiciliato in Palo Strada San Domenico, i quali han dichiarato che nel giorno nove del mese di settembre anno corrente alle ore venti è morta nella casa di sua abitazione sita alla Strada La piazza Dª Leonarda Catelina nata in Modugno di anni ottantasei di professione gentildonna domiciliata in Palo figlia del fu D. Nicola di professione domiciliat e della fu Dª Rosa Alfonso di anni di professione domiciliat e vedova del fu Don Francesco Savino

Per esecuzione della Legge ci siamo trasferiti insieme co' detti testimonj presso la persona defunta, e ne abbiamo riconosciuta la sua effettiva morte, abbiamo indi formato il presente atto, che abbiamo iscritto sopra i due registri, e datane lettura a' dichiaranti, si è nel giorno, mese, ed anno come sopra segnato da noi menoché dai Dichiaranti che han detto non saper scrivere

Cifra del Giudice delegato dal Presidente del Tribunale Civile.

Tommaso Frasca

FIGURE 8-19 **1832 death record of Leonarda Catelino, transcribed format.**

ACT OF DEATH.

Ordinal No. 145

In the year one thousand eight hundred thirty two, day *nine*
of the month of *September* at the hour of *twenty one*
Before us *Tommaso Frasca Mayor* and officer
of the Vital Records of the town of *Palo* District of *Bari*
Province of Terra di Bari , appeared *Domenico Yulgcis of*
Palo age *forty two* occupation *farmer*
citizen living *in Palo Silecchia Street* , and *Mauro Gru*
mo of Palo -
occupation *shoemaker* citizen living in *Palo San Domenico Street*
, whom both have declared that on day *nine*
of the month of *September* year *current*
at hour *twenty* — - -
at La Piazza Street - died at the *house of her residence*
D^a Leonarda Catelina
born in *Modugno*
age *eighty six* occupation *gentlewoman*
living *in Palo* daughter of *the late D. Nicola*
occupation - living
and of *D^a Rosa Alfonso* living age - -
occupation - - - living - - - - , *and widow of the late Don*

Francesco Savino - - -

According to the law we travelled together with these
witness to the house of the deceased person and we have witnessed her
effective death, we have then created the present act, that
we have written above two copies, we have read to the informants
on the day, month, and year above signed by us
but not by the informants who have stated that they don't know how to write

Signature of the delgated Judge of the
President of the Civil Court

Tommaso Frasca

FIGURE 8-20 **1832 death record of Leonarda Catelino, translated format.**

Data Extract Form

Stato Civile of Italy—Death Record of: **Leonarda Catelina**

Document Source

Microfilm: **1607421**	Title: **Stato Civile, Palo, Morti 1817-1841**
Year: **1832**	Document Number: **145**

Record Creation

Date: **9 September 1832 21:00**
Clerk: **Tommaso Frasca**
Place: **Palo**

Informant

	Informant 1	Informant 2
Name:	**Domenico Vulgcis**	**Mauro Grumo**
Birthplace:	**Palo**	**Palo**
Age:	**quarantadue (42)**	**settanta (70)**
Son/Dau of:		
Occupation:	**contadino**	**calzolaio**
Residence:	**Palo strada Silecchia**	**Palo Strada San Domenico**

Deceased

Name:	**Dª Leonarda Catelina**
Death Date:	**9 September 1832 20:00**
Place of Death:	**Palo strada La Piazza**
Birthplace:	**Modugno**
Age:	**ottantasei (86)**
Occupation:	**gentildonna**
Residence:	**Palo Strada La Piazza**
Father:	**fu D. Nicola**
Occupation:	
Residence:	
Mother:	**fu Dª Rosa Alfonso**
Occupation:	
Residence:	

Witnesses

	Witness 1	Witness 2
Name:		
Birthplace:		
Age:		
Son/Dau of:		
Occupation:		
Residence:		

Miscellaneous Notes

Researcher: **Lynn Nelson**　　　　　Date: **July 14, 1995**

FIGURE 8-21 **Completed Data Extract Form for the 1832 death record of Leonarda Catelino.**

CHAPTER NINE

Where to Find the Records

Now that you know which records you need and how to use them, you're ready to find the *Stato Civile*. There are four ways to obtain these documents. First, you may use the Family History Library and its branches. This is the best place to start because it is fast, easy, inexpensive and doesn't require traveling any great distances. This method will be the primary focus of this chapter.

The second method you may use to obtain records of the *Stato Civile* is correspondence. Performing your research via international correspondence is more difficult. You must know the correct place to write, write your letter in Italian, and hope that they still have the records. It is also more time-consuming. Responses may take weeks, months or never appear. Finally, this method is more expensive. In some situations, however, this may be the best option. The secondary focus of this chapter is how to perform your research through correspondence.

A third option is to take a trip to Italy and visit the appropriate offices and archives yourself. This method is very expensive and requires you to be very familiar with not only the Italian language, but with the culture. You could find that your investment in time and money for a trip like this ended up being fruitless. This option may be best combined with a vacation to Italy after you have exhausted the other options.

A fourth option is to hire a researcher to obtain the documents for you. This can become expensive but is easier than traveling to Italy yourself. This may be a good option to choose after you have exhausted the first two recommended strategies. Read the advertisements in genealogical journals to find a researcher who is experienced in Italian research. Ask for references and make sure you come

to an understanding of what you should expect to pay and what you should expect to get.

The Family History Library

The Family History Library, the greatest genealogical resource in the world, is operated by The Church of Jesus Christ of Latter-day Saints, also called the LDS church or, simply, the Mormons. Their religious ceremonies include "sealing" family members so that all may be together in the hereafter. The family members include not just immediate and extended family, but long-dead ancestors as well. In order to do this, they must first identify their ancestors through genealogical research.

Because genealogical information is very important to the LDS church, they have amassed a huge amount of genealogical data. For decades, they have traveled all over the world, microfilming vital records, books, public records and anything else of genealogical value. These films are stored in a great vault in a granite mountain in Utah. All of this data is available at the main Family History Library, located in Salt Lake City, as well as all branch Family History Centers, located all over the United States, Canada and worldwide.

The Library and its centers are open to the general public. You do not have to be a member of the church to use its resources. The staff is friendly, helpful and knowledgeable. The Family History Library is the resource that will allow you to climb your Italian family tree quickly, easily and without going abroad. The quantity and value of the records that are available through the Family History Library are just astounding!

Finding Your Local Family History Center

If you live in or around Salt Lake City, then you can use the main Library there. If not, you can use one of the thousands of Family History Centers located throughout the world. These centers have a permanent collection consisting of records of local interest. They allow you to borrow any microfilm or microfiche from the main Library in Salt Lake City. You can only view the films and fiche at the Family History Center. You cannot take them out of the facility. They have microfilm and microfiche readers, copiers, publications and genealogical supplies.

Since the Family History Library is a nonprofit organization, the fees charged are very reasonable; they are just enough to cover their costs. For example, to borrow a microfilm from the main Library for sixty days costs just $3.50 at my local Family History Center (these prices may vary from center to center). To use the resources in a Family History Center's permanent collection costs nothing! The Library also publishes many valuable booklets on a wide variety of genealogical topics that range in price from free to $.75.

To find your nearest Family History Center, use your local yellow pages to look up "Churches - The Church of Jesus Christ of Latter-day Saints." The churches with a Family History Center will have a listing for the center. If you cannot find one in the yellow pages, call the Library in Salt Lake City (800-346-6044) to ask for your nearest Family History Center.

Once you have located the nearest Family History Center, call to ask about operating hours. Ask if you need to schedule use of the computer. Some centers have only one computer and schedule blocks of time for its use.

The Family History Library Catalog

Your goal for your first visit to the Family History Center will probably be to determine which records they hold for your immigrant ancestor's Italian hometown. You will use the Family History Library catalog to accomplish this. The catalog is available on microfiche and on CD-ROM via the computer. I generally prefer the computer, but ask which one is most current. Sometimes the microfiche are updated on a more frequent basis than the CD-ROMs.

The CD-ROM catalog is organized by locality and by surname. For the purpose of determining which records are available for your Italian town of interest, you will use the locality search. You will be prompted for three things: 1) a town or parish, 2) a county or province (excepting Canadian provinces) and 3) a country, state of the United States, or Canadian province. Enter the name of the Italian town for the town; the Italian province name for the county/province option; and "Italy" for the country. For example, if you are interested in learning what records are available for the town of Palo del Colle in the province of Bari, Italy, you would enter "Palo del Colle" in the town/parish field, "Bari" in the county/province field, and "Italy" in the country field.

A list of record types is displayed with brief descriptions. For example, *Civil Registration, 1809 - 1865*, may be one line on the screen. We are mainly interested in the civil records at this time, but you may want to print out this list for future reference. Select the option for the civil records. If there are no civil records available for your town (unlikely, but possible), you will have to write to Italy to obtain the information. Writing to Italy is addressed in the next section of this chapter.

A detailed list of the civil registration records for your town will be displayed. Figure 9-1 shows an example of such a list for the town of Gravina di Puglia in the province of Bari. The top of the screen will show general information about these records, such as the format (33 reels of microfilm, 16mm), and a general description of the contents. Note that some of this is in English and some is in Italian.

The lower part of the display shows the type of record, the year ranges and the microfilm number. For example, the first entry is *Nati* (births) from 1809 through 1821 on microfilm number 1603603, item 2-5. If you were interested in obtaining this film you would use this microfilm number to order it. The reference to "item 2-5" means that there are other records contained on the same reel of film, but the 1809 - 1821 birth records are the second through fifth items on the microfilm. The other items on the film may be birth records from other towns, other records (marriage, death, etc.) from this town, or items from completely different time

```
AUTHOR
Gravina di Puglia (Bari).  Ufficio dello stato civile.

TITLE
Stato civile, 1809-1900.

PUBLICATION INFORMATION
Salt Lake City : Filmati dalla Genealogical Society of Utah, 1988-1990.

FORMAT
in 33 bobine di microfilm ; 16 mm.

NOTES
Microfilm dei registri originali nell'Archivio di Stato, Trani.
Microfilm di alta riduzione (42x).  Adoperate una macchina di
alto ingrandimento.
Annotazioni di morte filmati con:  Giovinazzo (Bari).  Ufficio dello
stato civile, e Grumo Appula (Bari).  Ufficio dello stato civile.

CONTENTS
I memorandum matrimoniali contengono informazione simile a quella nei
    notificazioni matrimoniali.
I documenti degli allegati per gli anni 1866-1896 per la provincia di
    Bari sono filmati tutti insieme.  Si trovano sotto:  Bari
    (Provincia).  Ufficio dello stato civile.  Il "record number" [CCF
    number] áe 732518.
Births, marriages, banns, marriage documents, deaths, miscellaneous
    documents, citizenship records.  The marriage memorandum contain
    the same type of information as the marriage banns.  Includes
    death notices added to birth records.
    The supplemental records for 1866-1896 are all filmed together under:
    Bari (Provincia).  Ufficio dello stato civile.  The record no. (CCF
    no.) is 732518.
Include indici.
```

		EUROPE FILM AREA
Nati	1809-1821	1603603 item 2-5.
Nati	1821-1828	1603574
Nati	1828-1834	1603575
Nati	1834-1839	1603576
Nati	1839-1845	1603577
Nati	1845-1851	1603578
Nati	1851-1859	1603579
Nati	1859-1865	1603617
Matrimoni	1809-1817	
Matrimoni	1818-1835	1603618
Matrimoni	1835-1848	1603619
Matrimoni	1848-1860	1603620
Matrimoni	1861-1865	1603621
Morti	1809-1816	
Morti	1816-1823, 1829-1837	1603622

FIGURE 9-1 **Listing from the Family History Library catalog for records of civil registration for the town of Gravina di Puglia, Bari, Puglia, Italy. (Reprinted by permission. Copyright 1987, 1995 by The Church of Jesus Christ of Latter-day Saints.)**

```
Morti            1837-1840, 1824-1828, 1841-1844 ---------------- 1603650
Morti            1844-1854 -------------------------------------- 1603651
Morti            1854-1864 -------------------------------------- 1603652
Morti            1864-1865 -------------------------------------- 1603653
    Atti diversi  1816-1865
    Memorandum,
    notificazioni 1862-1865
    Processetti    1862
Processetti      1862-1863 -------------------------------------- 1603654
Processetti      1863-1865 -------------------------------------- 1603655
Processetti      1865 ------------------------------------------- 1603656
                                                                     item 1
Nati             1866-1874 -------------------------------------- 1642287
                                                                     item 2-4.
Nati             1875-1885 -------------------------------------- 1642288
Nati             1885-1894 -------------------------------------- 1642289
Nati             1895-1900 -------------------------------------- 1642290
                                                                     item 1-2
Notificazioni 1866-1883 ----------------------------------------- 1660003
                                                                     item 2-4.
Notificazioni 1884-1900 ----------------------------------------- 1660004
                                                                     item 1-2
Matrimoni        1866-1880 -------------------------------------- 1660198
                                                                     item 3-4.
Matrimoni        1881-1900 -------------------------------------- 1660199
                                                                     item 1-2
Morti            1866-1873 -------------------------------------- 1692716
                                                                     item 2-3.
Morti            1874-1890 -------------------------------------- 1692717
Morti            1891-1900 -------------------------------------- 1692718
                                                                     item 1-2
Cittadinanze  1866-1900 ----------------------------------------- 1692977
                                                                     item 21
Annotazioni di morte   1866-1900 -------------------------------- 1692979
                                                                     item 2


THIS RECORD FOUND UNDER
    1. Italy, Bari, Gravina di Puglia - Civil registration
```

periods. By scanning the other microfilm numbers in this list we can see that this microfilm number does not appear anywhere else for this town, which means that the other items on this particular microfilm must be records from another town.

Notice that the first entry is for births from 1809 through 1821 and the second entry is for births from 1821 through 1828. The records for the year 1821 begin on one film and end on a different film. If you were looking for a birth record from 1821 you would probably order both films because the index for 1821 would be located only on one of these films. Sometimes when a year of records is split across films like this, the catalog may specify which month starts and ends on each microfilm (but not in this example).

The Family History Library catalog on microfiche contains the same type of listing as shown in Figure 9-1, but it is accessed sequentially because it is organized alphabetically, by country, province, and town. For example, to find this same listing you would use the microfiche by locality and look up Italy, Bari, Gravina di Puglia, Civil Registration.

Once you have found the catalog listing of records for your Italian town, print it out for future reference. The next step is to order the film or films of interest. You fill out an order form for each film, pay the fee, and in two to four weeks your film will be in. Now your ancestor hunting really begins!

Research by Correspondence

The Family History Library should be your first choice of research methods. However, there are some situations that may require you to write to Italy to pursue your Italian heritage. If the Family History Library has not filmed records from the town of your ancestors, then you must perform your research via correspondence. Or maybe they have filmed records for your town, but the time periods you need are not available. For example, I have ancestors from Caserta, but the civil records available from the Family History Library span the years 1809 through 1865. Since I needed to start my research with records from the late 1800s, I had to write to Italy to obtain the information necessary to get back to 1865, and then I was able to use the microfilms from the Family History Library.

If you have narrowed down your ancestor's birthplace to a province but still need to determine the town, you may have to write to Italy for the military records (see chapter five), because very few have been filmed by the Family History Library.

In any case, whatever your reasons for using correspondence to perform your research, be aware that this method requires patience. You will not get the immediate gratification that you can experience using microfilms from the Family History Library.

In order to insure success in your research via correspondence, you must follow three guidelines. First, you must know the location of the information that you need. Second, you must write your requests in Italian. Finally, you must know how to handle the administrative details, such as postage, international payments, etc. The rest of this chapter will cover these details.

Where to Write in Italy

There are different jurisdictions for different kinds of records. Some records can be found in more than one office. Before sending a letter, double-check the location of the record and the address. Below you will find specific advice on how to send for each major record type.

Vital Records

When the original birth, marriage and death records of the *Stato Civile* were created, two copies were made. One copy remained in the *Ufficio di Stato Civile* (the local town's office of the *Stato Civile*) and one copy was sent to the *Procura della Repùbblica* (district attorney) of the province. The local *Ufficio di Stato Civile* still retains the original copy of the records from the nineteenth century, while most of the records held by the *Procura della Repùbblica* are transferred to the *Archìvio dì Stato* (state archives) after seventy-five years. Many of the records held at the *Archìvio di Stato* have been microfilmed and are available at the Family History Library. Since two copies of the civil vital records were made (three, if you count the microfilms), there is a good chance that at least one still exists and that you can find it.

When writing to Italy for vital records, you will write to the local *Ufficio di Stato Civile*. Today, this same office still registers births, marriages and deaths, and issues the documents as needed, for example when a birth certificate is required to obtain a driver's license or passport. Because the older records are usually stored in a less accessible place than the modern records, and because your request for genealogical information has a lower priority than most of the other requests they receive (such as a citizen trying to obtain a passport), the clerks of the *Ufficio di Stato Civile* may delay responding to your requests. Be patient. You can make their task easier by writing in Italian (to be covered in the next section) and by following the guidelines suggested in the following section.

The address to which you will send your request will follow the format in the following example:

Ufficio di Stato Civile
Comune di Santa Maria Capua Vetere
81055 Santa Maria Capua Vetere (CE)
Italia

The first line indicates the Office of the Vital Records. The second line indicates the town. You would replace *Santa Maria Capua Vetere* with the name of your town of interest. The third line includes the postal code for the town, the name of the town and the name or abbreviation of the province.

You can find the postal code in an Italian gazetteer (discussed in chapter five) or call the Italian Consulate in New York City at (212) 737-9100. You can leave it out if you cannot find it, but I do not recommend it. The province name or abbreviation is very important since there may be many towns throughout Italy with the same name. A list of province abbreviations is provided in Figure 9-2.

Military Records

As discussed in chapter five, if you are unable to determine the hometown of your immigrant ancestor, but have narrowed it down to a particular province, you may use the military records to discover the town since they are organized at the province level. The military conscription records are stored at the *Archìvio di Stato*. There is one main *Archìvio di Stato* for each province (and several minor ones, called *sezióne*). Their addresses are listed in Appendix C.

Writing Your Request in Italian

Although many Italians can understand English, it is best to write your request in Italian. Anything that you can do to make the clerk's job easier increases your chance of obtaining a successful reply.

Appendix B contains an Italian Letter-Writing Guide. This guide provides you with common phrases and sentences used to request genealogical information in Italian. You can mix and match them to create your own custom letters. A sample letter is also provided for guidance.

Miscellaneous and Administrative Details

Sending your request in Italian and to the appropriate office are the two most important elements when performing your research through correspondence. However, there are some other miscellaneous and administrative details that are also important to your success.

Include All Known Information

When requesting a document for an ancestor, include as much information as possible about that ancestor. The name alone is not sufficient, since many people may have had the same name due to the Italian naming custom. Include the spouse's name and the parents' names, if known, and any approximate dates if the exact date of the record is unknown. If you simply ask for the birth record of Antonio Napoli born in the 1890s, the clerk may ignore your request because there could be dozens of records for that name and time period.

Type Your Request

It is better to type your request than to send a handwritten letter. Modern European handwriting can be a little different than North American handwriting. A typed letter eliminates any ambiguities. It is easier to read and looks more professional. Remember, anything that you can do to make the clerk's job easier increases your chances of receiving a successful reply.

Self-Addressed Return Envelope

Including a self-addressed return envelope is a small thing for you to do and one less thing for the clerk to do. It also insures that your address is correct. Do not place postage on this envelope (see return postage below) and don't forget to include "U.S.A." or "Canada" in the address.

Return Postage

Always include return postage with your request. For international mail, use International Reply Coupons (IRCs). They are available at the post office for about one dollar each. Enclose two IRCs with each request. Frequently, they will not be used and will be returned to you with the reply.

Province Abbreviations by Region

Abruzzo
- CH   Chieti
- AQ   L'Aquila
- PE   Pescara
- TE   Teramo

Basilicata
- MT   Matera
- PZ—Potenza

Calabria
- CZ   Catanzaro
- CS   Cosenza
- KR   Crotone*
- VV   Vibo Valentiä

Campania
- AV   Avelino
- BN   Benevento
- CE   Caserta
- NA   Napoli
- SA   Salerno

Emila-Romagna
- BO   Bologna
- FE   Ferrara
- FO   Forli
- O   Modena
- PR   Parma
- PC   Piacenza
- RA   Ravenna
- RE—Regio Emilia
- RN—Rimini

Fruili-Venezia Guilia
- GO   Gorizia
- PN   Pordenone
- TS   Trieste
- UD   Udine

Lazio
- RF   Frosoinone
- LT   Latina
- RI   Rieti
- ROMA Roma
- VT Viterbo

Liguria
- GE   Genova
- IM   Imperia
- SP   La Spezia
- SV   Savona

Lombardia
- BG   Bergamo
- BS   Brescia
- CO   Como
- CR   Cremona
- LC   Lecco*
- LO   Lodi*
- MN   Mantova
- MI   Milano
- PV   Pavia
- SO   Sondrio
- VA   Varese

Marche
- AN   Ancona
- AP   Ascoli Piceno
- MC   Macerata
- PS   Pesaro

Molise
- CB   Campobasso
- IS   Isernia

Piedmonte
- AL   Allessandria
- AS   Asti
- BI   Biella*
- CN   Cuneo
- NO   Novara
- TO   Torino
- VB   Verbano-
- Cusio-Ossola*
- VC   Vercelli

Puglia
- BA   Bari
- BR   Brindisi
- FG   Foggia
- LE   Lecce
- TA   Taranto

Sardegna
- CA   Cagliari
- NU   Nuoro
- OR   Oristano
- SS   Sassari

Sicilia
- AG   Agrigento
- CL   Caltanissetta
- CT   Catania
- EN   Enna
- ME   Messina
- PA   Palermo
- RG   Ragusa
- SR   Siracusa
- TP   Trapani

Toscana
- AR   Arezzo
- FI   Firenze
- GR   Grosseto
- LI   Livorno
- LU   Lucca
- MS   Massa-Carrara
- PI   Pisa
- PT   Pistoia
- PO   Prato*
- SI   Siena

Trentino-Alto Adige
- BZ   Bolzano
- TN   Trento

Umbria
- PG   Perugia
- TR   Terni

Valle D'Aosta
- AO   Aosta

Veneto
- BL   Belluno
- PD   Padova
- RO   Rovigo
- TV   Treviso
- VE   Venezia
- VR   Rerona
- VI   Vicenza

* Added in 1993

Figure 9-2 **Italian province abbreviations by Region.**

Payment in Lire

You will not be sending any form of payment with your initial request because you don't know how much it will cost. But if the document that you requested is found, you may receive a reply requesting payment in *lire*. They may charge up to 10,000 *lire* per document (approximately $6.50 U.S., based on the current exchange rates at the time of this writing). They may charge nothing at all, or something in between.

Most major banks can issue cashier's checks in foreign currencies. Even easier, use Ruesch International at (800) 424-2923. They will send you international drafts in Italian *lire* for any denomination for a three-dollar service charge.

Legal Versus Nonlegal Paper

Extracts of documents issued by the *Ufficio di Stato Civile* can be in two formats, *in carta legale* (legal paper) or *in carta libera* (nonlegal paper). This distinction is similar to certified versus noncertified documents in the United States. For offical purposes, such as obtaining a passport, a certified document *in carta legale* is required. A special stamp is placed on the document, for which an additional charge is made. For genealogical purposes you should request the document *in carta libera* to save money.

A Case Study

CHAPTER TEN

Searching for Francesco; a Step-By-Step Example

Now that you know the steps to follow in your genealogical research, how to understand the Italian vital records, and where to find them, you're ready to perform your own research. This chapter pulls all these guidelines together into a step-by-step example that illustrates the actual process.

For this case study, we will be searching for information about Francesco Savino, husband of Vincenza Angelastro. We first learned of Francesco from the marriage and birth record of his daughter, Arcangela. We also identified some siblings of Arcangela by reviewing the indices for other children of Francesco Savino and Vincenza Angelastro. From each of these documents, we obtained some genealogical information about Francesco. We learned that both he and Vincenza were born in the town of Gravina di Puglia. Based on his ages on these documents, we determine that he was born between 1808 and 1814. From the records of their children, we estimate that Francesco and Vincenza were married before 1836 (the birth year of the oldest known child).

The first record we should seek for Francesco is his marriage record. We start with the marriage record instead of the birth record for a very important reason; we don't know the names of Francesco's parents. If we were to search for his birth record, we would be likely to find many documents for Francesco Savino because this is a common name. How will we know which one is our Francesco if we do not know the names of his parents? Knowing the name of his wife, we can obtain the marriage record first, solving this initial problem by supplying us with the names of his parents.

The first thing we must do is establish a specific research goal by answering the four *W*s:

- Who: Francesco Savino and Vincenza
  Angelastro
- What: Marriage record
- Where: Gravina di Puglia, Italy
- When: before 1836

We determined the where by assumption. Traditionally, marriages have always taken place in the birth town of the bride. Because they were both born in Gravina di Puglia, and because they continued to live in Gravina and raise their family there, this is the most likely town in which to search for their marriage record.

We will use the Italian Genealogy Research Checklist in Figure 10-1 to guide us in our research. A blank form is available in Appendix D for you to copy. Use one form for each research goal.

According to the Checklist, our next task is to determine the location of this marriage document so that we may obtain it. Our first choice is the Family History Library. We check their catalog to see what records are available for the town of Gravina di Puglia, Italy.

Figure 9-1 (in the last chapter) shows a Family History Library Catalog listing for Gravina di Puglia. By reviewing this listing we see that marriage records from 1809 through 1900 are available. We need the film that contains the marriage records from 1835 and earlier, so we should order microfilm number 1603618, which contains marriage records for Gravina from 1818 through 1835. Notice that the year 1835 is split across two films. This means that the index for 1835 may be on the first film (if the index is located before the records) or the second film (if the index follows the records). We could order both films, but because we are seeking a document from 1835 or earlier, we will probably find the marriage record of Francesco and Vincenza on

Italian Geneology Research
Checklist

I. Establish a Goal

    Who: **Francesco Savino and Vincenza Angelastro**

    What: **Marriage record**

    Where: **Gravina di Puglia, Bari, Apulia, Italy**

    When: **before 1836**

II. Determine Document Location

    A. First, check the Family History Library

        1. check the FHL catalog for the town's records

        2. Determine microfilm number: **1603618**

        3. Order film. Date ordered: **04 Jan 1996**

        4. Film has arrived. Date due: **10 Feb 1996**

    B. If not available in Family History Library

        1. Write letter to Italy

III. Perform Research

    A. Review microfilm

        1. Find required year

        2. Find index for year

        3. Search index for ancestor

        4. Find document

        5. Complete data extraction form for document

        6. Photocopy document

        7. Update research log to record successful or unsuccesful research

        8. Review all the indices on microfilm for surnames

        9. Make note of siblings and relatives

        10. Update your research log to record the names for which you searched

    B. Or Review Extract from Italy

        1. Update your research log to record success or failure.

IV. What Have I Learned

    A. List new information discovered in this research process

	Ancestor	Ancestor	Ancestor	Ancestor
Who:	Francesco S	Vincenza A		
What:	Birth	Birth		
Where:	Gravina	Gravina		
When:	abt 1810	abt 1815		
Misc.:	Parents	Parents		

V. Fill Out New Research Checklists for Above Goals

FIGURE 10-1 **Sample Italian Genealogy Research Checklist for finding the marriage record of Francesco Savino and Vincenza Angelastro.**

the earlier film. We can always order the second film later if we need to do so.

We fill out the Family History Library order form, pay the appropriate fee and within two to four weeks are notified of the arrival of our film. The regular short-term film loan is sixty days, so make a note of the due date on the Checklist. If we are not finished with the microfilm by its due date, we may renew it for an additional six months.

This film contains marriage records from 1818 through 1835. Since we are interested in the records from 1835 and earlier, it would be most efficient to start with 1835 and work backwards until we find the marriage record of Francesco Savino and Vincenza Angelastro.

Each year of records begins with a cover page, like the one shown in Figure 10-2 (translated in Figure 10-3). Information on the cover is not always filled in. In this example, the district and town names are not entered. Often you will even find the year missing on the cover page. Don't confuse the year mentioned in the boilerplate at the end of the cover page (1808 in this example) with the year of the records (1831). The year 1808 refers to the year of the Royal Decree, which dictates the maintenance of the records. If you cannot tell the year or town from the cover page, simply look at the first record following the cover. The first sentence or two should provide this information.

Once we have found the location of the records for the desired year on the microfilm, we next look for the index to that year. The index may be located before the records (just after the cover page) or following the records. It is possible that there is no index at all, in which case we have to review all the records.

For our example here, there is an index following each year's records. The records for 1835 are continued on a different film, along with its index, so we will skip 1835 for now and come back to it only if we don't find what we're looking for in the prior years. We review the index for each year, starting with 1834, working backwards. We look under the section for the letter *S* for Savino if the index is by last name or under the section *F* for Francesco if the index is by first name. Marriage records are always indexed by the groom's name. Also, check the end of the index in case the clerk writing the index ran out of room and placed additional entries at the end. When we reach the index for 1831, we find the page shown in Figure 10-4.

Entry number 60 in this index lists Savino Francesco and Angelastro Vincenza. We found them! The index also shows the names of their parents. Even though the parents' names are also listed in the actual marriage document, make a note of the names written here in case the ones in the document are illegible. Francesco's parents are Gius^e (Savino) and Arcangela Pappalardi. Vincenza's parents are Michele (Angelastro) and Giacoma Gramegna. The index shows the marriage date to be September 18. By reviewing the first column of numbers in the index, we determine that these are just chronological numbers, not page or document numbers; therefore we must use the date of September 18 to locate the actual marriage document on film.

The marriage records on this film are *atti della solènne proméssa di celebrare il matrimònio*, which means they were created shortly before the actual marriage. Since the marriage occurred on September 18, we will try to find the last record created on September 18 and search backwards from there to find the marriage document for Francesco and Vincenza. Remember, the documents appear in the order in which they were created (chronologically) and the *proméssa* may have been created several days before the marriage ceremony.

Using this method we quickly locate the desired marriage record. Figures 10-5, 10-6 and 10-7 show the first page of this document in three different formats. Figures 10-8, 10-9 and 10-10 show the second page of this document in the same three formats. These are the same three formats used for document examples in chapter eight. For the rest of this discussion refer to the second and third formats. Then, as you did with the document examples in chapter eight, practice your translation and paleography skills by trying to read the first format on your own, using the second and third formats for assistance.

The document was created on September 17, one

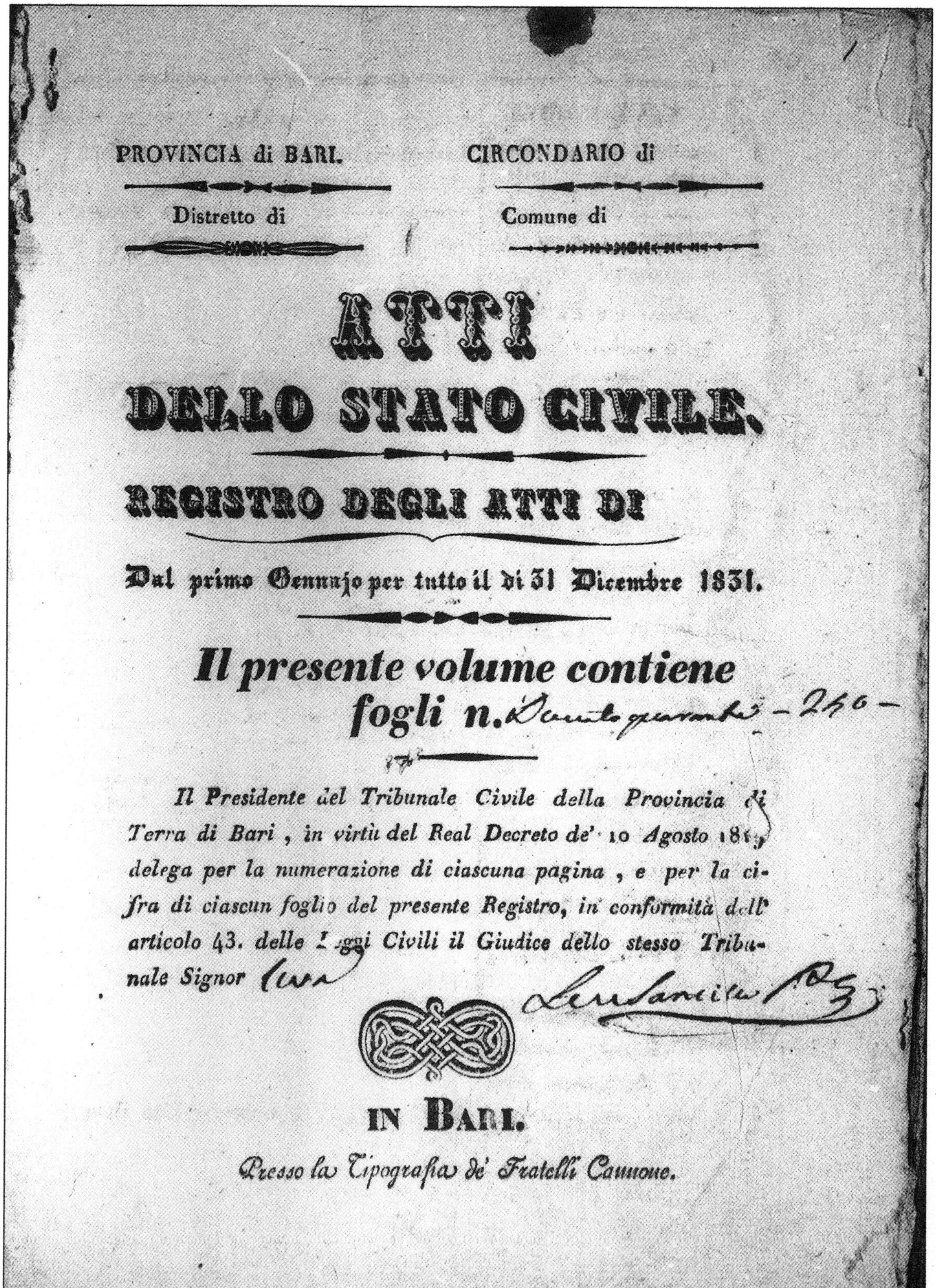

PROVINCIA di BARI.   CIRCONDARIO di

Distretto di   Comune di

ATTI
DELLO STATO CIVILE.

REGISTRO DEGLI ATTI DI

Dal primo Gennajo per tutto il dì 31 Dicembre 1831.

Il presente volume contiene
fogli n. *Sento quaranta* – 240 –

Il Presidente del Tribunale Civile della Provincia di
Terra di Bari, in virtù del Real Decreto de' 10 Agosto 18..
delega per la numerazione di ciascuna pagina, e per la cifra di ciascun foglio del presente Registro, in conformità dell'
articolo 43. delle Leggi Civili il Giudice dello stesso Tribunale Signor *(un*

IN BARI.

Presso la Tipografia de' Fratelli Cannone.

FIGURE 10-2 Cover page from the 1831 marriage records of Gravina di Puglia, original Italian format. (Photograph courtesy of the Family History Library of The Church of Jesus Christ of Latter-day Saints)

PROVINCE of BARI

District of

TERRITORY of

Town of

ACTS
OF THE VITAL RECORDS

REGISTER OF THE ACTS OF

From the first of January to the 31 of December 1831.

The present volume contains
pages n. *two hundred forty* – 240 –

The president of the Civil Tribunal of the Province of
Terra di Bari, by virtue of the Royal Decree of August 10, 1808
authorized by the enumeration of each page, and by the signature
on each page of the present register, in conformance with
article 43. of the Civil Laws the magistrate of the same Tribu-
nal Mister Uva

IN BARI.

Printing Press of the Cannone Brothers

FIGURE 10-3 **Cover page from the 1831 marriage records of Gravina di Puglia, translated English format.**

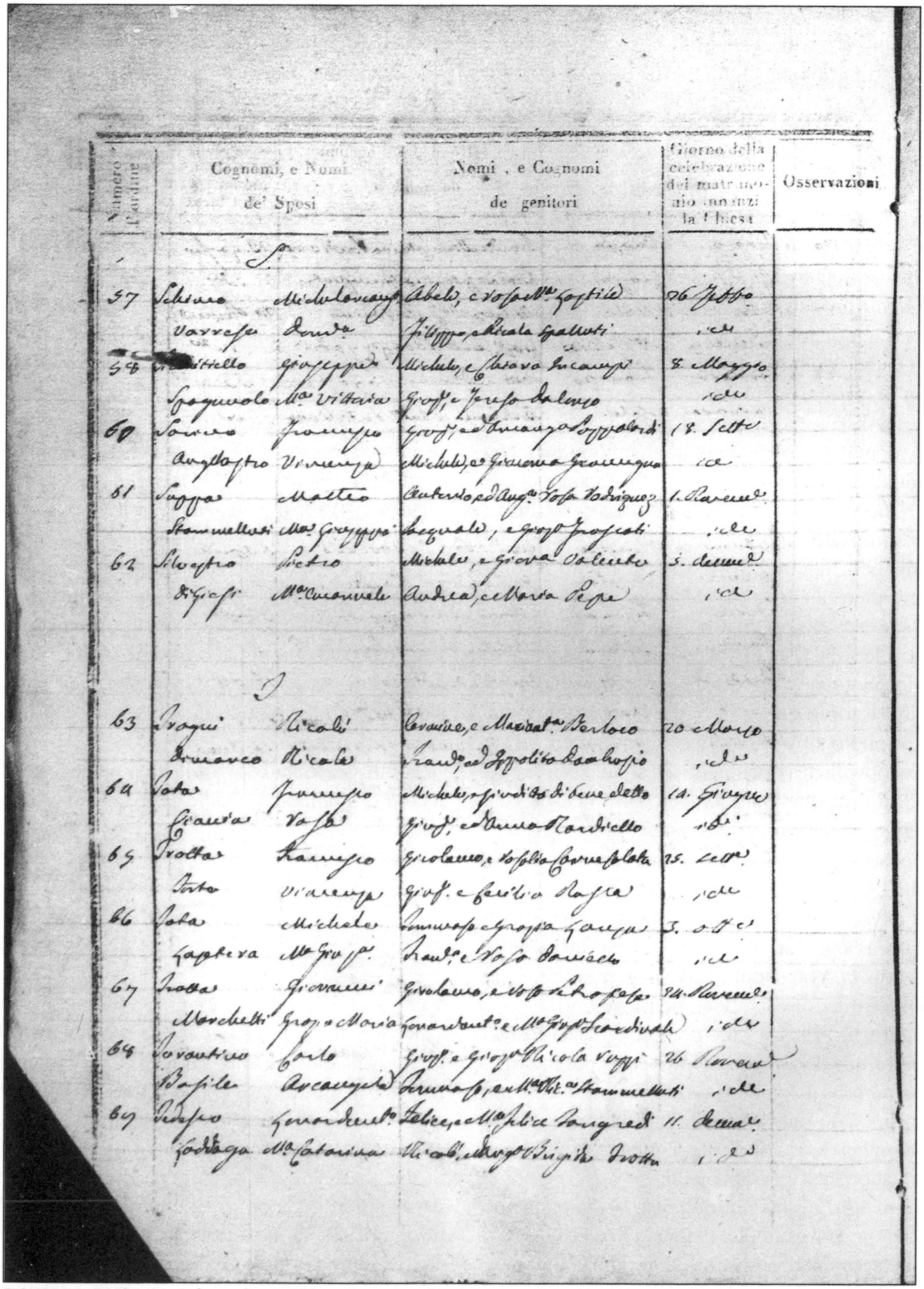

FIGURE 10-4 **Index page from the 1831 marriage records of Gravina di Puglia. (Photograph courtesy of the Family History Library of The Church of Jesus Christ of Latter-day Saints)**

day before the actual marriage occurred. On this day, Francesco was twenty-one years old, giving an estimated birth year of 1810. This is probably the most accurate birth year that we have for him, because this document is the oldest record we have seen that mentions him (and therefore closest in time to the actual event of his birth). Also, he reported the information here, not an informant as on his children's birth records.

This marriage record is a typical example of an *atto della proméssa di celebrare il matrimònio*. What is important to us about this particular document is that we have found additional information about Francesco Savino and Vincenza Angelastro. We now know the names of their parents, so we have identified a new generation, adding two new Italian surnames to our heritage; this branch of our family tree has just doubled. We have confirmed their birthplaces and approximate birth years. The information required to pursue their birth records is now all available.

The next tasks on the Checklist (Figure 10-1) are to complete the Data Extract Form for this document and to photocopy the document, if possible. Most Family History Centers have the equipment necessary to photocopy microfilms. Even though we are photocopying this document, we should still extract the data onto the Data Extract Form because the quality of the photocopy is usually not as good as it appears on the microfilm reader. Later on, when reading your photocopy, you may have to refer back to your completed Data Extract Form for clarification. Blank Data Extract Forms are included in Appendix D. You should make copies of these and complete one for each document you find.

Figure 10-11 shows the completed Data Extract Form for this document. Always enter the information exactly as it appears on the original document, in Italian. You may write the translation next to it in parentheses, if you wish. You should write the information exactly as it appears because it is possible to make a mistake during the transcription and translation. For example, the age of *trentadue* (32) may be accidentally transposed during your translation to 23 instead of 32. Writing the original data on the form eliminates this potential problem.

The next step on our Research Task Checklist (step III, A, 7) reminds us to record the status of this research goal. In this case, we were successful in finding the desired document. If we were not successful, we would still record the fact that we searched this film for the marriage record of Francesco Savino and Vincenza Angelastro so that we wouldn't later search the same film again.

As long as we have this microfilm on loan, we may as well review all available indices for our surnames of interest (step 8). We may find marriage records for the siblings of Francesco and Vincenza, from which we may obtain more information about their parents. Fill out a Data Extract Form for any relatives you find (step 9). Also, update your research log to show that you searched these indices for these surnames (step 10).

Section IV of the Research Task Checklist provides a place to list the newly learned information. This helps us determine what our next research goal will be by pointing out the four *W*s. In this case we confirmed the birthplace and approximate birth year for both Francesco Savino and Vincenza Angelastro, along with the names of their parents. Now we can create two new research goals: Find their birth records.

For this case study, we will next pursue the birth record of Francesco. Figure 10-12 shows our new Research Task Checklist.

Our new goal is:

- Who: Francesco Savino
- What: Birth record
- Where: Gravina di Puglia
- When: about 1810

Review the list of *Stato Civile* records available for Gravina in the Family History Library catalog in Figure 9-1 (in the previous chapter). Film number 1603603 contains births for the years 1809 through 1821 as items two through five on this film. That means that there are other items on this particular microfilm in addition to Gravina births from 1809 through 1821. These items may contain other types of documents, other years or even records from other towns. By glancing through the column of microfilm numbers in the catalog listing, we don't

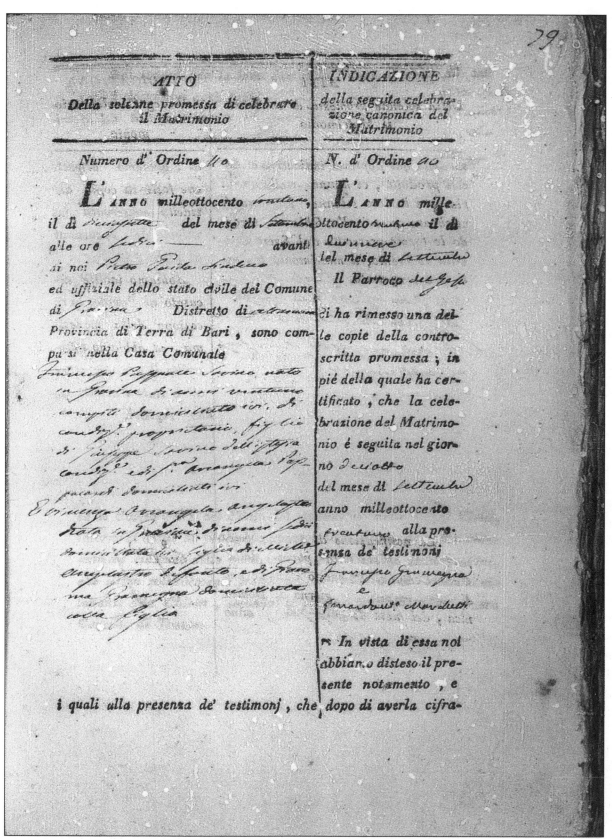

FIGURE 10-5 **1831 marriage record of Francesco Savino and Vincenza Angelastro, first page, original format. (Photograph courtesy of the Family History Library of The Church of Jesus Christ of Latter-day Saints)**

ATTO

Della solenne promessa di celebrare il Matrimonio

Numero d' Ordine 40

L'ANNO milleottocento *trentuno* il dì diciassette *del mese di* settembre alle ore sedici avant ai noi: Pietro Guida Sindaco ed ufficiale dello stato civile del Comune di Gravina Distretto di Altamura Provincia di Terra di Bari, sono comparsi nella Casa Comunale

Francesco Pasquale Savino nato in Gravina di anni ventuno compiuti domiciliato ivi, di condiz° proprietario, figlio di Giuseppe Savino della stessa condiz° ed S.ra Arcangela Pappalardi domiciliata ivi

E Vincenza Arcangela Angelastro nata in Gravina di anni sedici domiciliata ivi, figlia di Michele Angelastro defunto, e di Giacoma Gramegna domiciliata alla figlia

i quali alla presenza de' testimonj, che

INDICAZIONE

della seguita celebrazione canonica del Matrimonio

N. d' Ordine 40

L'ANNO mille-ottocento trentuno il dì diciannove del mese di settembre Il Parroco del Gesu ci ha rimesso una delle copie della contro-scritta promessa; in piè della quale ha cer-tificato, che la cele-brazione del Matrimo-nio è seguita nel gior-no diciotto del mese di settembre anno milleottocento trentuno alla pre-senza de testimonj Francesco Gramegna e Lonardant° Marchetti

In vista di essa noi abbiamo disteso il pre-sente notamento, e dopo di averla cifra-

FIGURE 10-6 **1831 marriage record of Francesco Savino and Vincenza Angelastro, first page, transcribed format.**

ACT	NOTICE
Of the solemn promise to celebrate Matrimony	*of the following celebration of the canonical Marriage*

<table>
<tr><td>

Number 40

The year one thousand eight hundred *thirty one*
day *seventeen* of the month of *September*
at hour *sixteen* before

us   *Pietro Guida Mayor*

and officer of the vital records of the Town

of *Gravina*   District of *Altamura*

Province of Terra di Bari, appeared

in the Town Hall

*Francesco Pasquale Savino born
in Gravina age twenty one
attained, living there,
occupation property owner, son
of Giuseppe Savino of the same
occupation and Mrs Arcangela Pap-
palardi living there*

*And Vincenza Arcangela Angelastro
born in Gravina age sixteen
living there, daughter of Michele
Angelastro deceased, and of Giaco—
ma Gramegna living
with her daughter.*

who in the presence of witnesses, who

</td><td>

Num. 40

The year one thousand
eight hundred *thirty one* day
nineteen
of the month of *September*
The Rector *of Jesus*

has returned to us one of
the copies of the here-
written promise; at the
bottom of which he has cer-
tified, that the cele-
bration of the marriage
occurred on day
eighteen
of the month of *September*
year one thousand eight hundred
thirty one in the pre-
sence of witnesses

*Francesco Gramegna
and
Lonardant° Marchetti*

In view of this we
have written the pre-
sent notation, and
after having sign-

</td></tr>
</table>

FIGURE 10-7 **1831 marriage record of Francesco Savino and Vincenza Angelastro, first page, translated format.**

find this same film number, which means the other items are not for Gravina di Puglia, but for another town.

We order the film, and when it arrives we locate the second item on the film. Items are generally separated by some blank film and a card with information about the filmer and the date and place it was filmed. Next we find the cover page for the Gravina births. An example of the cover page for 1810 is shown in Figure 10-13 (in English in Figure 10-14). Notice that the year of 1810 is written out in words, making it harder to find. It would be easy to confuse the other years that are written as numbers on this page with the year for the records if you're not careful.

Our plan is to review the indices on this microfilm, beginning with 1809. However, for this particular film, the first few years are not indexed. This is a fairly common occurrence for the early years of 1809 and 1810. We are going to have to review all the documents for these years, which can be time-consuming. Before we start, however, we can make this task easier by reviewing a couple of the documents to understand their layout. Once we determine where the name of the baby is in the document and locate the names of the parents, we can quickly skim through the documents, searching for Francesco Savino.

We find Francesco in 1810, as shown in Figure 10-15. We can be fairly certain that this is him because the parents' names here match the names on Francesco's marriage record. However, it is possible that this could be a sibling of Francesco's that died in infancy; it was very common to rename a child after a deceased sibling. A margin notation about Francesco's marriage to Vincenza would confirm this, however margin notations were not common on these earliest records. We search the other years and do not find another Francesco Pasquale Savino born of Giuseppe and Arcangela Pappalardi, so we can be fairly certain we have our ancestor.

Figures 10-15, 10-16 and 10-17 show Francesco's birth record in three different formats. Again, the first format is the original document. The second format replaces the handwritten Italian script with typed Italian script, and the third format replaces the Italian with English, showing how the document translates. Use all three formats to assist you in learning to read and understand Italian civil birth records.

Francesco Savino's birth record is a fairly typical example of a birth record from the earliest years of the *Stato Civile*. It contains slightly less information than the birth records in later years (like the birth record in chapter eight). For example, there is no indication of the baptism, although it does mention the parish in which Giuseppe lives.

The record was written on the twenty-fourth of May, 1810, and the birth occurred *ièri*, which means yesterday, so Francesco was born on the twenty-third of May. Notice the surname of the informant (who is the father, in this case) is written as Savini, not Savino. On Francesco's marriage record (and those of his siblings) the name was Savino. Why is it Savini here? There are three possible explanations. It could be a completely different person with a similar name. Sometimes surnames undergo an evolution over time, where the spelling or pronunciation of the name changes. This could be an example of such an evolution. Most likely, the clerk simply made a mistake. Savini and Savino were both common names in this town (see the witness named Savini in this document) and the clerk may have just written Giuseppe's name wrong. We can confirm this by reviewing this same film for other children of Giuseppe and Arcangela to see how his name is written on those documents and comparing the place of residence to make sure that it is the same couple. This example illustrates the importance of always looking for slight variations of your surname when searching the records.

We follow the remaining steps on our Checklist, including filling out a Data Extract Form for this document (Figure 10-18), and searching the other years on the film for any birth records of Francesco's siblings. We do find a few siblings and confirm that the Giuseppe's last name is spelled Savino, so the Savini on Francesco's birth record is just an error.

Using the new information that we have discovered, we can now create new research goals. This process, where each successful research goal begets new goals, can continue until you have exhausted

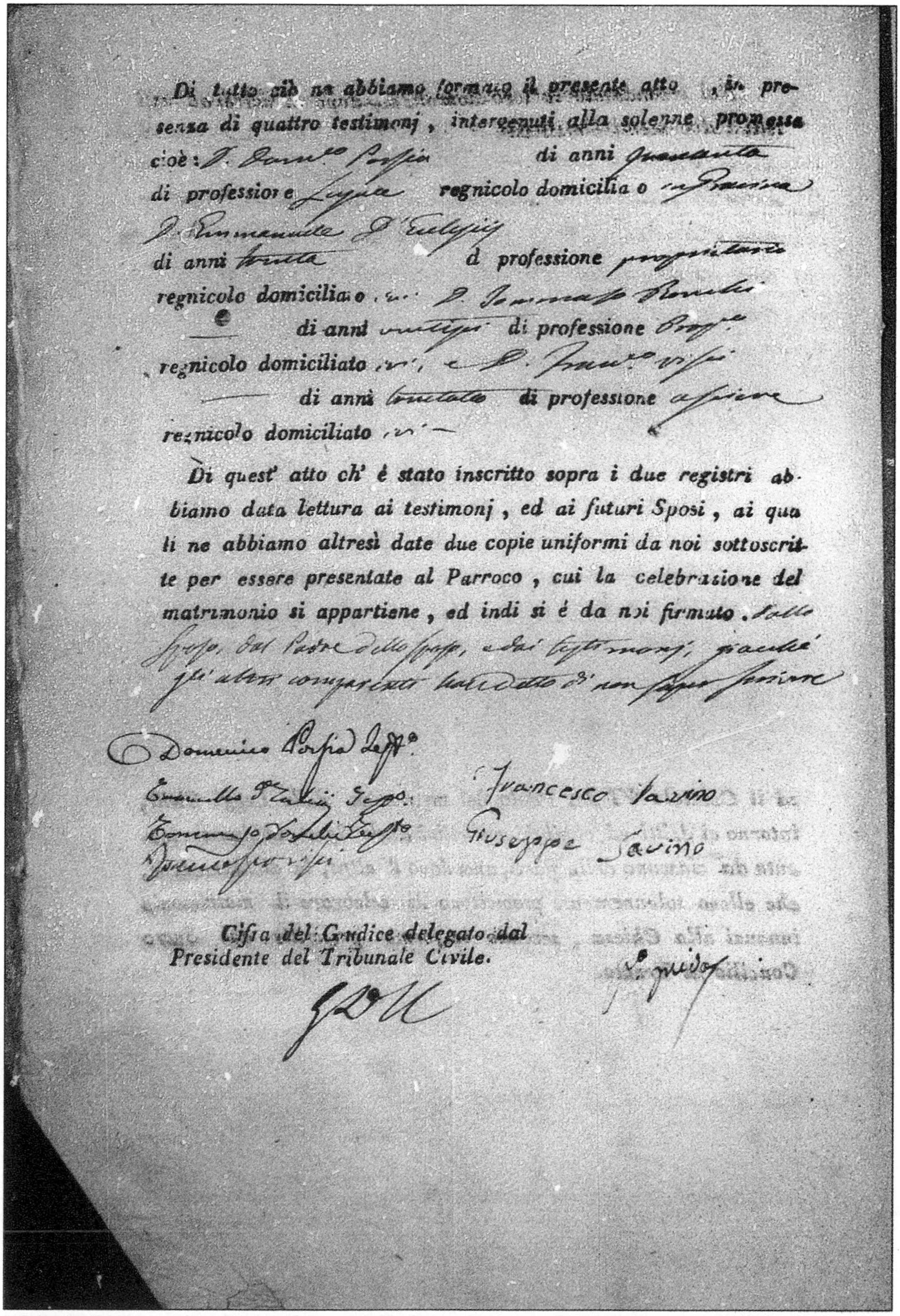

FIGURE 10-8 **1831 marriage record of Francesco Savino and Vincenza Angelastro, second page, original format.**
(Photograph courtesy of the Family History Library of The Church of Jesus Christ of Latter-day Saints)

Di tutto ciò qui abbiamo formato il surgente atto , in presenza di quattro testimonj, intervenuti alla solenne promessa
cioè: D. Dom° Porsia di anni quaranta
di professione Legale regnicolo domiciliao in Gravina
D. Emmanuele D'Eulisiis
di anni trenta d professione proprietario
regnicolo domiciliao ivi. D. Tommaso Ronabi
——— di anni ventisei di professione Prop°
regnicolo domiciliato ivi. e D. Fran.° Visci
——— di anni trentotto di professione assicure
regnicolo domiciliato ivi —

Di quest' atto ch' è stato inscritto sopra i due registri abbiamo data lettura ai testimonj, ed ai futuri Sposi, ai qua
li ne abbiamo altresì date due copie uniformi da noi sottoscritte per essere presentate al Parroco, cui la celebrazione del
matrimonio si appartiene, ed indi si è da noi firmato. dello
Sposo, dai Padre dello Sposo, e dai testimoni, giacche
gli altri comparenti han detto di non saper scrivere

Domenico Porsia Test.°
Emmanuelle d'Eulisii Test.°
Tommaso Ronabi Test.°
Francesco Visci

Francesco Savino

Giuseppe Savino

Cifra del Giudice delegato dal
Presidente del Tribunale Civile.

GDU

P. Guida

FIGURE 10-9 **1831 marriage record of Francesco Savino and Vincenza Angelastro, second page, transcribed format.**

From all this we have created the present act , in the presence of four witnesses, in attendance at the solemn promise
namely: *Mr. Domenico Porsia* age *forty*
occupation *Lawyer* citizen living *in Gravina*
Mr Emmanuele D'Eulisiis
age *thirty* occupation *property owner*
citizen living *there.* *Mr. Tommaso Ronabi*
— age *twenty six* occupation *property owner*
citizen living *there,* and *Mr Fran.co Visci*
— age *thirty eight* occupation *insurer*
citizen living *there* —

From this act that was written above in two registers we
have read to the witnesses, and to the future spouses, to whom
we have also given two exact copies signed by us
to be presented to the Rector, who will unite them in
in the marriage ceremony, and then is given our signature. *of the*
Groom, of the father of the Groom, and of the witnesses, since
the other participants have stated they don't know how to write

Domenico Porsia Witness
Emmanuelle d'Eulisii Witness **Francesco Savino**
Tommaso Ronabi Witness **Giuseppe Savino**
Francesco Visci

Signature of the delegated Judge of the
President of the Civil Court.

GDU *P. Guida*

FIGURE 10-10 **1831 marriage record of Francesco Savino and Vincenza Angelastro, second page, translated format.**

Data Extract Form

Stato Civile of Italy—Marriage Record of: **Francesco Savino**

and: **Vincenza Angelastro**

Document Source

Microfilm: **1603618**	Title: **Stato Civile, Gravina Matrimoni 1818-1835**
Year: **1831**	Document Number: **40**

Record Creation

Date: **17 September 1831 16:00**

Clerk: **Pietro Guida, sindaco**

Place: **Gravina**

Marriage Date: 19 SEP 1831

	Groom	Bride
Name:	Francesco Pasquale Savino	Vincenza Arcangela Angelastro
Birthplace:	Gravina	Gravina
Age:	ventuno	sedici
Occupation:	proprietario	
Residence:	Gravina	Gravina
Notes:		
Father:	Guiseppe Savino	Michele Angelastro, defunto
Occupation:	stressa (same—proprietario)	
Residence:	Gravina	Gravina
Mother:	Sʳᵃ. Arcangela Pappalardi	Giacoma Gramegna
Occupation:		
Residence:	Gravina	alla figlia

Witnesses

	Witness 1	Witness 2
Name:	D. Domenico Porsia	D. Emmanuele D'Eulisiis
Birthplace:		
Age:	quaranta (40)	trenta (30)
Son/Dau of:		
Occupation:	Legale	proprietario
Residence:	Gravina	Gravina

	Witness 3	Witness 4
Name:	D. Tommaso Ronabi	D. Francesco Visci
Birthplace:		
Age:	ventisei (26)	trentotto (38)
Son/Dau of:		
Occupation:	proprietario	assicure
Residence:	Gravina	Gravina

Miscellaneous Notes

Researcher: **Lynn Nelson**   Date: **March 4, 1995**

FIGURE 10-11 **Completed Data Extract Form for the 1831 marriage record of Francesco Savino and Vincenza Angelastro.**

Italian Geneology Research
Checklist

I. Establish a Goal
Who: **Francesco Savino**
What: **Birth record**
Where: **Gravina di Puglia, Bari, Apulia, Italy**
When: **abt 1810**

II. Determine Document Location
A. First, check the Family History Library
   1. check the FHL catalog for the town's records
   2. Determine microfilm number: **1603603**
   3. Order film. Date ordered: **01 Feb 1996**
   4. Film has arrived. Date due: **12 Mar 1996**
B. If not available in Family History Library
   1. Write letter to Italy

III. Perform Research
A. Review microfilm
   1. Find required year
   2. Find index for year
   3. Search index for ancestor
   4. Find document
   5. Complete data extraction form for document
   6. Photocopy document
   7. Update research log to record successful or unsuccesful research
   8. Review all the indices on microfilm for surnames
   9. Make note of siblings and relatives
   10. Update your research log to record the names for which you searched
B. Or Review Extract from Italy
   1. Update your research log to record success or failure.

IV. What Have I Learned
A. List new information discovered in this research process

	Ancestor	Ancestor	Ancestor	Ancestor
Who:	Giuseppe S	Arcangela P	Giuseppe S	
What:	Marriage record		Birth	
Where:	Gravina		Gravina	
When:	bef 1810		abt 1786	
Misc.:				

V. Fill Out New Research Checklists for Above Goals

FIGURE 10-12 **Sample Italian Genealogy Research Checklist for finding the birth record of Francesco Savino.**

the records of the *Stato Civile* by finding ancestors that were born or married before the records began in 1809.

For this example, another goal could be to find the birth record of Vincenza Angelastro (Francesco's wife), on this same film. Also, we could pursue the marriage record of Francesco's parents, Giuseppe Savino and Arcangela Pappalardi, which we may assume occurred before 1810 since Francesco was born May 1810. The records of the *Stato Civile* begin in 1809, so unless they were married in 1809, we will not find a marriage record for them in these records. In that case, there are two things we may do.

For events prior to 1809, church records are the next logical avenue to pursue. Although the focus of this book is the *Stato Civile*, the civil vital records of Italy, the final chapter contains a section called Where to Go From Here. This section briefly reviews how to continue your genealogical research beyond the existence of the *Stato Civile*.

Before you give up on the *Stato Civile*, there is something else you may do to continue your family tree back two or even three additional generations. Use the *Atti di Morti* (death records). In our example above, although Francesco's parents were born and married before the initiation of the civil vital

records, they died after 1810. In fact, we know that they died after 1831 since they were both living at the time of Francesco's marriage. Using the process of elimination we can narrow down the dates of their deaths to a small window of time and then search for their death records. Once we find their death records, we will have the names of their parents, whose death records we could search for next. This process can continue until you find ancestors that died before 1809, so it is a method of squeezing a few additional generations out of the *Stato Civile*.

One warning, however, about using death records to identify ancestors. Of all the vital records, death records contain the least amount of information. In order to identify your ancestor, the record must have the name of the spouse of the deceased. Without this information you cannot be sure it is your ancestor. Even with this information, it is possible that there is more than one couple with the names of your ancestors. With very common names, you should look at the address or any other information on the record in order to confirm that you have found your ancestor.

Using this method, you can easily identify ancestors that were born as far back as the early to mid-1700s.

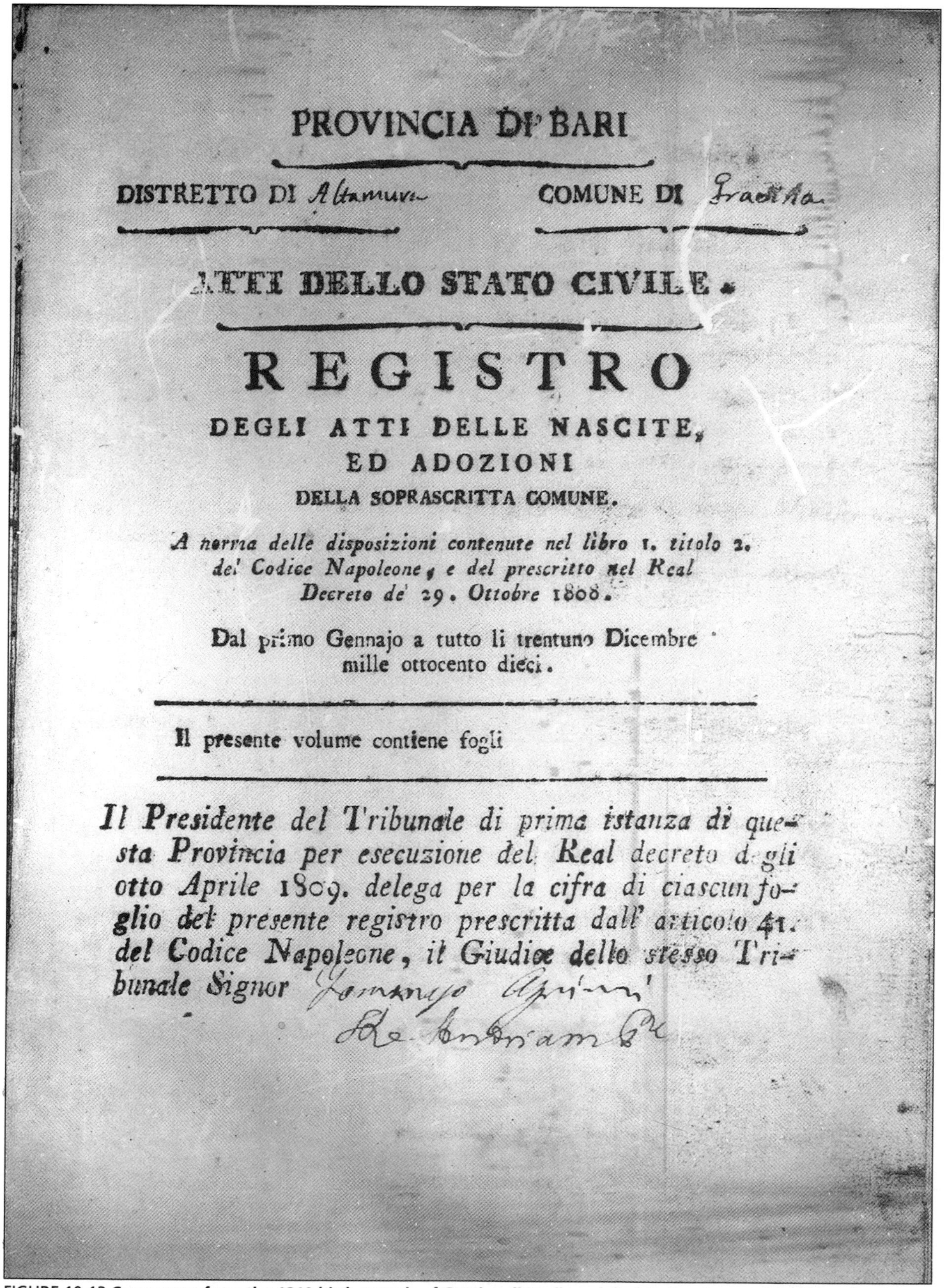

PROVINCIA DI BARI

DISTRETTO DI *Altamura*   COMUNE DI *Gravina*

ATTI DELLO STATO CIVILE.

REGISTRO

DEGLI ATTI DELLE NASCITE,
ED ADOZIONI
DELLA SOPRASCRITTA COMUNE.

*A norma delle disposizioni contenute nel libro 1. titolo 2.
del Codice Napoleone, e del prescritto nel Real
Decreto de' 29. Ottobre 1808.*

Dal primo Gennajo a tutto li trentuno Dicembre
mille ottocento dieci.

Il presente volume contiene fogli

Il Presidente del Tribunale di prima istanza di questa Provincia per esecuzione del Real decreto degli
otto Aprile 1809. delega per la cifra di ciascun foglio del presente registro prescritta dall' articolo 41.
del Codice Napoleone, il Giudice dello stesso Tribunale Signor *Domenico Apicella*

FIGURE 10-13 **Cover page from the 1810 birth records of Gravina di Puglia, original Italian format. (Photograph courtesy of the Family History Library of The Church of Jesus Christ of Latter-day Saints)**

PROVINCE OF BARI

DISTRICT OF *Altamura*   TOWN OF *Gravina*

ACTS OF THE VITAL RECORDS

REGISTER

OF THE ACTS OF BIRTHS,
AND ADOPTIONS

OF THE ABOVE WRITTEN TOWN

According to the provisions contained in book I. title 2.
of the Napoleon Code, and of the prescript of the Royal
Decree of October 28, 1808

From the first of January to the thirty first of December
one thousand eight hundred and ten.

The present volume contains pages

The president of the Tribunal of the first instance of this
Province by execution of the Royal decree of the
eighth of April 1809, authorized by the signature on each page
of the present register prescribed by article 41
of the Napoleon Code, the magistrate of the same Tri-
bunal Mister *Tommaso Apriani*

FIGURE 10-14 **Cover page from the 1810 birth records of Gravina di Puglia, translated English format.**

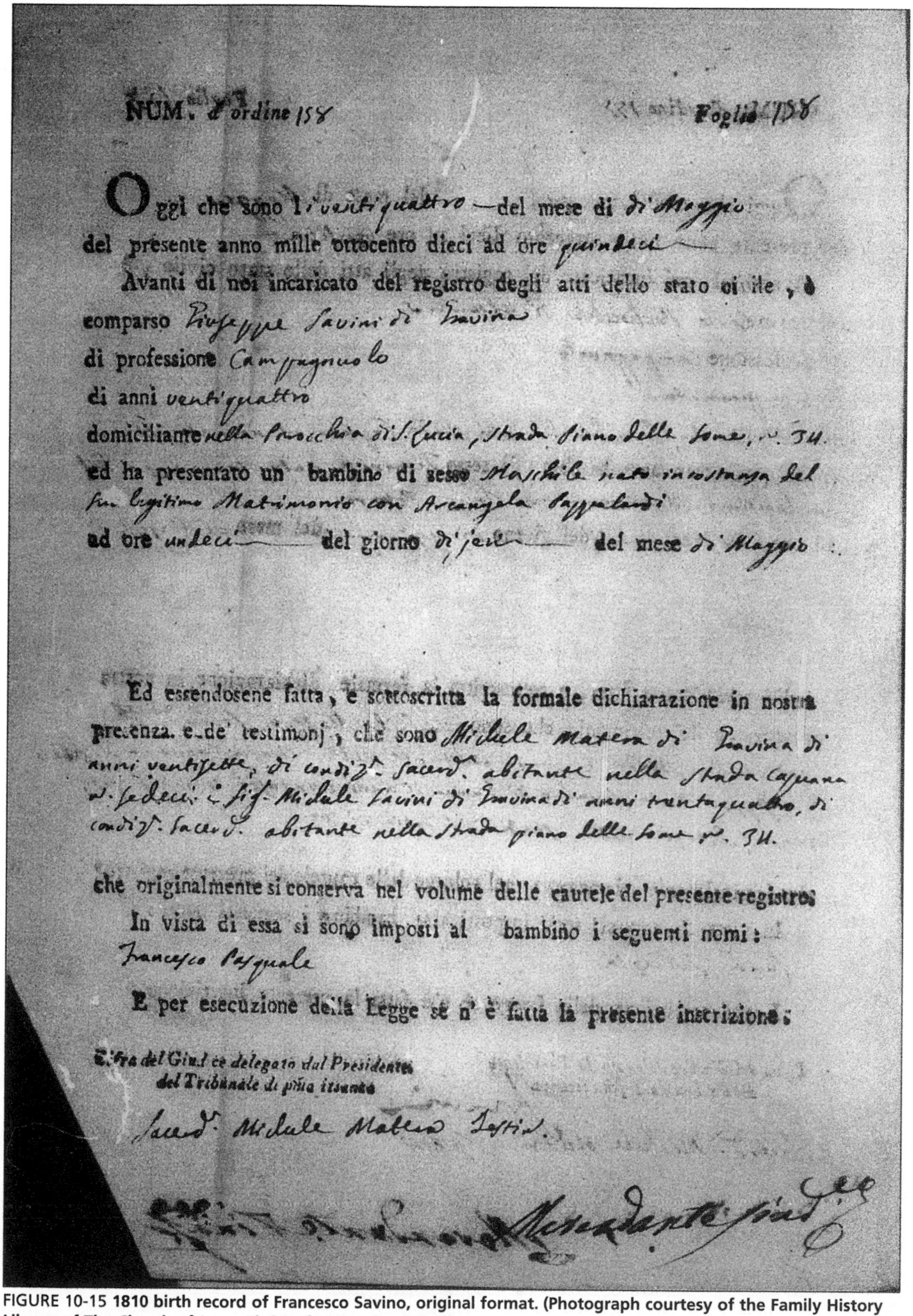

NUM. d'ordine 158   Foglio 158

Oggi che sono li ventiquattro — del mese di di Maggio
del presente anno mille ottocento dieci ad ore quindici —
    Avanti di noi incaricato del registro degli atti dello stato civile, è
comparso Giuseppe Savini di Travina
di professione Campagnuolo
di anni ventiquattro
domiciliante nella Parocchia di S. Lucia, Strada Piano delle Fosse, N. 34.
ed ha presentato un bambino di sesso Maschile nato in costanza del
suo legitimo Matrimonio con Arcangela Pappalardi
ad ore undeci — del giorno di jeri — del mese di Maggio

    Ed essendosene fatta, e sottoscritta la formale dichiarazione in nostra
presenza e de' testimonj, che sono Michele Matera di Travina di
anni ventisette, di condiz. Sacerd. abitante nella Strada Cajenna
N. Sedeci e Sig. Michele Savini di Travina di anni trentaquattro, di
condiz. Sacerd. abitante nella Strada piano delle Fosse N. 34.

che originalmente si conserva nel volume delle cautele del presente registro
    In vista di essa si sono imposti al bambino i seguenti nomi:
Francesco Pasquale
    E per esecuzione della Legge se n' è fatta la presente inscrizione:

E.ffa del Giud ce delegato dal Presidente
    del Tribunale di pria istanza

Sacerd. Michele Matera Testi.

FIGURE 10-15 **1810 birth record of Francesco Savino, original format. (Photograph courtesy of the Family History Library of The Church of Jesus Christ of Latter-day Saints)**

Oggi che sono li ventiquattro   del mese di di maggio

del presente anno mille ottocento dieci ad ore quindici

Avanti di nel incaricato del registro degli atti dello stato civile, è

comparso Giuseppe Savini di Gravina

di professione campagnuolo

di anni ventiquattro

domiciliante nella Parocchia di S. Lucia, strada Piano delle Some, N° 34

ed ha presentato un bambino di sesso maschile nato in costanza del

suo legitimo matrimonio con Arcangela Pappalardi

ad ore undici   del giorno di ieri   del mese di maggio

Ed essendosene fatta, e sottoscritta la formale dichiarazione in nostra

presenza e de' testimonj, che sono Michele Matera di Gravina di

anni ventisette di condiz°. sacerd°. abitante nella strada capriana

n°. sedici e Sig° Michele Savini di Gravina di anni trentaquattro di

condiz°. sacerd°. abitante nella strada piano delle some n°. 34.

che originalmente si conserva nel volume delle cautele del presente registro:

In vista di essa si sono imposti al bambino i seguenti nomi:

Francesco Pasquale

E per esecuzione della Legge se n' è fatta la presente inscrizione:

Firma del Giud ce delegato dal Presidente
del Tribunale di pria istanza

Sacerd° Michele Matera Testim°:

FIGURE 10-16 **1810 birth record of Francesco Savino, transcribed format.**

Today *the twenty fourth* of the month of *of May* of the present year one thousand eight hundred ten at hour *fifteen*

Before us officers of the registration of the acts of the vital records, appeared *Giuseppe Savini of Gravina*

occupation *peasant*

age *twenty four*

residing *in the Parish of St. Lucia, on street Piano delle Some N° 34*

has presented a baby of gender *masculine born in conjugality of his legitimate marriage with Arcangela Pappalardi*

at hour *eleven* of the day *yesterday* of the month *of May*

And having been made, and undersigned the formal declaration in our presence and of the witnesses, who are *Michele Matera of Gravina age twenty seven, occupation priest living on Capriana Street n° sixteen, and Mr. Michele Savini of Gravina age twenty four occupation priest living on Piano delle Some street N° 34*

The original of which is preserved in the volume of the present register

In view of this they are giving the baby the following names:

Francesco Pasquale

And for execution of the law the present inscription is made:

Seal of the delgated Judge of the President of the Tribunal of the first instance

Priest Michele Matera Witness

FIGURE 10-17 1810 birth record of Francesco Savino, translated format.

Data Extract Form

Stato Civile of Italy—Birth Record of: **Francesco Savino**

Document Source

Microfilm: **1603603**	Title: **Stato Civile, Gravina, Nati 1809-1821**
Year: **1810**	Document Number: **158**

Record Creation

Date: **24 May 1810**
Clerk:
Place:

Informant

Name: **Giuseppe Savini**	Age: **ventiquattro**
Birthplace: **Gravina**	Son/Dau of:
Occupation: **campagnuolo**	Residence: **strada Piano delle Some #34**

Parents

	Mother	Father
Name:	Arcangela Pappalardi	informant
Birthplace:		
Age:		
Dau/Son of:		
Occupation:		
Residence:		
Notes:		

Child

Name: **Francesco Pasquale**	Sex: **Maschile**
Birthdate: **ieri (23 May 1810)**	Birthplace: **Gravina**
Baptism Info:	
Notes:	

Witnesses

	Witness 1	Witness 2
Name:	Michele Matera	Michele Savini
Birthplace:	Gravina	Gravina
Age:	ventisette (27)	trentaquattro (34)
Son/Dau of:		
Occupation:	sacerdote	sacerdote
Residence:	strada capriana no seidici	strada piano delle some no 34

Margin Notations

Miscellaneous Notes

parocchia di S. Lucia

Researcher: **Lynn Nelson**   Date: **September 7, 1995**

FIGURE 10-18 **Completed Data Extract Form for the 1810 birth record of Francesco Savino.**

Conclusions

CHAPTER ELEVEN

Other Research Options

Some Interesting Miscellaneous Research

Researching Italian civil vital records to identify your ancestors is the backbone of discovering your Italian heritage. But there are a few other interesting projects you can pursue that will increase the enjoyment of your ancestor hunting. These projects will give you a feel for where and how your ancestors lived, and they will enable you to better understand your Italian heritage.

Obtain a Photo of Your Immigrant Ancestor's Ship

The Steamship Historical Society of America has a huge collection of photographs of the ships that carried our immigrant ancestors to North America. You may order these photographs in varying sizes. Their address is:

Steamship Historical Society of America
University of Baltimore Library
1420 Maryland Avenue
Baltimore, MD 21201

When you write to them, be sure to include the name of the ship, the name of the shipping line, and the year of your ancestor's immigration (ships changed their names quite frequently). They will send you an order form showing you what is available and the various photographic options.

Maps of Your Ancestral Homeland

Maps are an interesting addition to your collection of genealogical documents. They show the location of small towns in reference to larger towns, present an idea of the geography of the area (did your ancestor live in the mountains? on the shore? etc.), and provide the locations of local churches and other interesting features.

You can obtain maps of Italy in varying degrees of detail from good bookstores and map specialty stores. But, most of these maps are modern road maps at a scale that doesn't show much detail. A great map for Italian ancestor hunters is available from the Library of Congress in Washington, DC.

The *Grande Carta Topografià Del Régno D'Itàlia* is a map series (277 sheets) created shortly after the final unification of Italy. The scale is only 1:100,000 (about 1.7 miles per inch) and shows a great deal of detail. For example, railroad tracks, train stations and streetcar lines are shown. The roadways are classified as major roads, country roads, mule paths, cow paths and footpaths. Even more interesting, the land outside the towns is marked with the names of the landowners. Imagine my surprise to find several parcels of land with the names of some of my ancestors!

You may obtain oversized photocopies of these maps from the Library of Congress for only a few dollars for each 36″ × 18″ sheet. Write to the Geography and Map Division at the address below and request an order form for this map series. They will send you a graphic index, which is a map of Italy overlaid with a grid showing the locations of the 277 sheets in the map series, and an order form.

Library of Congress
Geography and Map Division
Washington, DC 20540-4650

Become an Italian Citizen

If either of your parents were born in Italy, you may be eligible to maintain dual citizenship. However, you must have been born before your mother or father became a naturalized American citizen. For more information, contact:

Italian Consulate
690 Park Avenue
New York, NY 10021
(212) 737-9100

Learn More About Your Ancestral Hometown

Most cities in Italy, even some of the smallest towns, have attractions of historical, cultural and natural interest. These attractions are often publicized in the form of tourist brochures and booklets. You can often obtain detailed maps, pamphlets containing photographs, and other literature about your immigrant ancestor's hometown by writing to the tourist bureau of its province. The tourist bureau is usually located in the provincial capital city. The address to use should follow this format:

Ente Provinciale del Turismo
70125 Bari, ITALIA

You will replace the postal code and the name of the provincial capital city with those of your province. You will find the postal codes for the provincial capitals in Appendix C, which lists the addresses of the archives. You may write your request in English, since this office serves tourists.

Join an Organization

There are several organizations for people interested in their Italian heritage. By becoming a member of such an organization, you meet people sharing your interest, receive publications containing interesting and valuable information, and you may even learn something that leads you to a long lost ancestor.

One such organization, POINT (Pursuing Our Italian Names Together), consists of several thousand members who are interested in their Italian genealogy. Members contribute lists of their ancestors' surnames, along with their regions, provinces and towns. This information is indexed and published in an annual directory. You may find some of your Italian surnames in this directory, and if these names are listed for the same town as your immigrant ancestor, you may have found a relative. Many members have found distant, unknown cousins through the POINT directory.

POINT also publishes a quarterly journal that is a source of interesting and valuable information for the Italian ancestor hunter. There are also regional groups of POINT members that hold regular meetings and participate in special events.

The dues for membership in POINT are currently $30 a year. The dues include the Annual Surname Directory and four issues of the quarterly journal. The address is:

POINT
P.O. Box 2977
Palos Verdes, CA 90274

Some other organizations of interest are:

Italian Genealogical Group of New York
7 Grayon Dr.
Dix Hills, NY 11746

Italian Genealogical Society of America
P.O. Box 8571
Cranston, RI 02920-8571

Where to Go From Here

This book provides the practical information that you need to discover your Italian ancestors by using the *Stato Civile* of Italy. These civil vital records only go back as far as 1809, so once you have pursued your Italian heritage back to ancestors that were born before that time, what next? Is it possible to go back even further?

Yes! Long before Napoleon instituted the *Stato Civile*, the Council of Trent mandated the churches to maintain records of all christenings, marriages and deaths. Some of these records go back as far as the 1500s. The existence of many of these records is in question, because they were never centralized, only one copy was created, and they were stored in places like church basements, where time and poor conditions have deteriorated them. And, relatively few church records have been filmed by the Family History Library. These old records were all handwritten following no particular format, and were written in Latin, in an Italian dialect, or a combination. They are hard to find and hard to read.

Despite all these problems, it is possible to continue your Italian family tree by using Italian church records. The processes of finding and reading these records is beyond the scope of this book. If you wish to pursue this avenue, an excellent book is available that focuses on ecclesiastical and other Italian records. The procedures discussed in *Italian*

Genealogical Records, by Trafford R. Cole, are the next logical steps for you to follow. This book emphasizes records that are only available in Italy and explains how to find them, either through correspondence or by traveling to Italy to perform the research yourself.

An alternative to researching the church records yourself is to hire a professional genealogist who specializes in Italian records. There are several companies that use experienced researchers who live in Italy. Look for a professional in the advertisements of genealogical journals. Make sure you ask for references and make it clear that you are interested in Italian records created prior to 1809.

Italian Word Lists

Cardinal Numbers

uno	one
due	two
tre	three
quattro	four
cìnque	five
sèi	six
sètte	seven
òtto	eight
nòve	nine
dièci	ten
ùndici	eleven
dódici	twelve
trédici	thirteen
quattórdici	fourteen
quìndici	fifteen
sédici	sixteen
diciasètte	seventeen
diciòtto	eighteen
diciannòve	nineteen
vénti	twenty
ventuno	twenty-one
ventidue, etc.	twenty-two, etc.
trénta	thirty
quaranta	forty
cinquanta	fifty
sessenta	sixty
settanta	seventy
ottanta	eighty
novanta	ninety
cènto	one hundred
duecènto, etc.	two hundred, etc.
mille	one thousand
duemila	two thousand
tremila, etc.	three thousand, etc.

Days of the Week

lunedì	Monday
martedì	Tuesday
mercoledì	Wednesday
giovedì	Thursday
venerdì	Friday
sàbato	Saturday
doménica	Sunday

Ordinal Numbers

primo	first
secóndo	second
tèrzo	third
quarto	fourth
quinto	fifth
sèsto	sixth
sèttimo	seventh
ottavo	eighth
nono	ninth
décimo	tenth
undicèsimo	eleventh
dodicèsimo	twelfth
tredicèsimo	thirteenth
quattordicèsimo	fourteenth
quindicèsimo	fifteenth
sedicèsimo	sixteenth
diciassettèsimo	seventeenth
diciottèsimo	eighteenth
diciannovèsimo	nineteenth
ventèsimo	twentieth
trentèsimo	thirtieth
quarantèsimo	fortieth
cinquantèsimo	fiftieth
sessantèsimo	sixtieth
settantèsimo	seventieth
ottantèsimo	eightieth
novantèsimo	ninetieth
centèsimo	one hundredth
millèsimo	one thousandth
pròssimo	next

penùltimo	next to last	città	city, town
ùltimo	last	cognóme	surname
		comesopra	as stated above
Months of the Year		comune	town
gennàio	January	cón	with
febbràio	February	condizióne	occupation
marzo	March	consènso	consent
aprile	April	cugino(a)	cousin
màggio	May	da	from, of
giugno	June	decèsso	deceased
lùglio	July	defunto	deceased
agòsto	August	degli	of the
settèmbre	September	dei	of the
ottóbre	October	della	of the
novèmbre	November	di	of
dicèmbre	December	dichiarante	informant
		dichiarato	declared
General Genealogical Terms		diocèsi	diocese
a	to, at	domani	tomorrow
abbiamo	we have	domiciliato	residing
abitazióne	home	dòn	sir
addì	on the day of	dònna	lady
altro	other, next	dòpo	after
anche	also, too	e	and
anni	years, age	è	is
anno	year	ed	and
antenato	ancestor	estratto	extract
antimeridiano	antemeridian, A.M.	età	age
atto	act, record	famìglia	family
ava	grandmother	fanciulla	girl
avanti	before	fanciullo	boy
avo	grandfather	figli	children
bambino(a)	baby	figlia	daughter
battésimo	baptism	figlio	son
battezzato(a)	baptized	firma	signature
bisnònna	great-grandmother	fratèllo	brother
bisnònno	great-grandfather	frazióne	hamlet
capofamìglia	head of the family	fu	was, deceased
casa	house	gemèllo(a)	twin
cattedrale	cathedral	genitóri	parents
cattòlica	catholic	giórno	day
cèlibe	unmarried male	gli	the (plural)
che	which, what	ha	was
chièsa	church	i	the (plural)
circa	about	ièri	yesterday
circondàrio	district, territory	ignòto	unknown

il	the	padrino	godfather
illegìttimo	illegitimate	parenti	relatives
in	in, on, at	parròcchia	parish
ìndice	index	pàrroco	rector, priest
ivi	there	patèrna	paternal
la	the	pàtria	of one's homeland
legìttimo	legitimate	per	for, by, to
lo	the	più	more
lóro	they, them	pomeriggio	afternoon
lui	him	prefètto	prefect
luògo	place	prète	priest
ma	but	professióne	occupation
madre	mother	progenitóre	ancestor
maggióre	majority, elder	proietto	orphan
marito	husband	pròssimo	next
matèrna	maternal	provìncia	province
matrimònio	marriage	pubblicazióni	wedding banns
mattina	morning	quadrisàvola	great-great-great grandmother
mése	month		
mòglie	wife	quadrisàvolo	great-great-great grandfather
mòrto(a)	dead, died		
nàscita	birth	quèl, quèlla	that
nati	births	quèsto(a)	this
natività	birth, nativity	regiòne	region
nativo(a)	native	registro	register
nato(a)	born	residènte	resident
negli	in the	richièsta	request
nei	in the	sècolo	century
nel, nella	in the	séra	evening
neonato(a)	newborn	sèsso	sex, gender
noi	us, we	sòno	are
nòme	name	sorèlla	sister
non	not, no	sottoscritto	undersigned
nònna	grandmother	spòsa	wife, bride
nònno	grandfather	sposato(a)	married
notificazióne	wedding banns	spòsi	spouses
nòtte	night	spòso	husband
nùbile	unmarried female	stato civile	vital records
numero	number	stato	were
o	or	su, sua	his, hers
odièrno	this day	suddétto	aforesaid
òggi	today	tàvola alfabèctica	index
óltre	in addition to	testimòne	witness
óra	hour	trisàvola	great-great grandmother
óre	hours	trisàvolo	great-great grandfather
padre	father	ufficiale	officer, official

ufficio	office	cocchière	coachman
un, una	a	coltellinàio	cutler, knifesmith
uòmo	man	commerciante	merchant
védova	widow	commésso	shop clerk
vèdovo	widower	conciatóre	tanner
zìa	aunt	construttóre	builder
zìo	uncle	contadino	peasant farmer
		cucitrice	seamstress

Common Occupations

agricoltóre	farmer	dottóre	doctor
albergatóre	inn keeper	droghière	grocer
albergatrice	inn keeper	ebanista	cabinetmaker
arrotino	knife grinder	erbivéndolo	produce monger
artigiano	craftsman	fabbricante	manufacturer, builder
assessóre	councilman	fabbro	blacksmith
attendante a casa	housekeeper	falegname	carpenter
avvocato	lawyer	fattóre	farm manager
barbière	barber	ferraro	blacksmith
barilào	cooper	filatrice	spinner
beccàio	butcher	fochista	stoker, fireman
becchino	sexton, gravedigger	fornàio	baker
bettolière	tavern keeper	fruttaiuolo	fruit monger
bidèllo	janitor, caretaker	fruttivèndolo	fruit monger
boaro	stableman	gelatàio	ice cream maker
boscaiòlo	woodcutter	gendarme	policeman
bottàio	cooper	gentildonna	gentlewoman
bottegàio	shopkeeper	gentiluomo	gentleman
bottegante	shopkeeper	giornalièro	day laborer
bovaro	stableman	guàrdia	guard
bracciale	laborer	guardiano	warden, watchman
bracciante	laborer	impotènte	disabled
bucatàia	washwoman	inbianchina	whitewasher
burràio	dairyman	infermièra	nurse
caffettière	coffee house keeper	ingegnère	engineer
cafone	peasant	insegnante	teacher
calzolàio	shoemaker	lanino	wool worker
camerièra	waitress, chambermaid	lattonàio	tinsmith
campagnòlo	peasant farmer	lattonière	tinsmith
capo	head, leader, boss	legale	lawyer
cappellàio	hat maker	legnaiulo	wood cutter
carabinièro	policeman	levatrice	midwife
carbonàio	coalman	loccandiera	innkeeper
carradóre	cartmaker, wheelwright	macchinista	railroad engineer
carrozzàio	carriage maker	macellàio	butcher
casalinga	housewife	maèstro	teacher, master
civile	middle-class person	magnano	locksmith
		maniscalco	blacksmith

marinàio	sailor	servànte	servant
mèdico	doctor	servànte	gunner
mendico	beggar	servitóre	servant
mercante	merchant	sindaco	mayor
mercanteéssa	merchant	soldato	soldier
merciàio	notions peddler	spaccalégna	wood cutter
minatóre	miner	stagnàio	tinsmith
mondina	rice weeder	stagnino	tinsmith
mugnaio	miller	stallière	stableman
mulattière	mule driver	stiratóre	ironer, presser
mulinaro	miller	stiratrice	ironer, presser
muratòre	bricklayer, mason	stracciaiòlo	ragman
negoziante	shopkeeper, merchant	tabaccàio	tobacconist
notàio	notary	tablitóre	tailor
ombrellàio	umbrella maker	tablitrice	tailor
operàio	workman	tagliapiètre	stone cutter
orciolàio	potter	tagliatóre	cutter
orologiàio	watchmaker, clockmaker	tavernière	tavernkeeper
ortolano	truck farmer	tappezzière	upholsterer, paperhanger
òste	innkeeper	terrazzano	land worker, villager
ostéssa	innkeeper	tessitóre	weaver
ostètrica	midwife	tessitrice	weaver
paesano	peasant	tintóre	dyer
panettière	baker	vasàio	potter
panieràio	basket weaver	vaticale	water vendor
pàrroco	rector, parson, priest	venditóre	seller, vendor
pastàio	pasta maker	veterinàrio	veterinarian
pasticcière	pastry maker	vetràio	glass maker
pastóre	shepherd, pastor	vetturale	driver
pensionato	retired	vetturino	carriage driver
pescatòre	fisherman	vigile del fuoco	fireman
pescivènaddo	fishmonger	vignaiòlo	vine dresser
pittóre	painter	villano	peasant
pizzicàgnola	grocer, sausage dealer	violinista	violinist
pollaiòlo	poultry keeper	viticoltore	wine grower
possidènte	property owner	zappatóre	hoer
prète	priest	zoccolàio	shoemaker
pretóre	judge, magistrate		
proprietàrio	owner, property owner		
ricamatrice	embroidress		
sacerdòte	priest		
sagrestano	sexton		
saponière	soapmaker		
sarto	tailor		
scalpellino	stone cutter		
sèrva	servant		

Male Names

Alessandro	Alfonso	Andrea
Angelo	Antonio	Attilio
Bartolomeo	Battista	Benedetto
Beniamino	Bernardo	Biaggio
Carlo	Carmelo	Carmine
Cataldo	Cesaro	Cosimo

Cristiano

Daniele   Domenico   Donato

Emanuelle   Ercole

Fabrizio   Fedele   Federico
Felice   Ferdinando   Filippo
Francesco

Gabriele   Gaetano   Gennaro
Gerardo   Geremia   Giacinto
Giacomo   Giambattisto Giorgio
Giovanni   Girolamo   Giuseppe
Gregorio   Guido

Ignazio   Isidoro

Lazzaro   Leonardo   Lonardo
Lorenzo   Luca   Luigi
Marco   Mario   Martino
Martire   Matteo   Mattia
Mauro   Michele

Nicola   Nicolo   Nunzio

Onofrio   Oranzo   Osvaldo

Paolo   Pasquale   Pietro
Pompeo

Raffaele   Renato   Roberto
Rocco   Roderico
Sabino   Salvatore   Santo
Saverio   Simone   Stefano

Teodoro   Tommaso

Ugo

Vincenzo   Vito   Vittorio

Female Names
Agata   Agnesa   Alba
Alfonsa   Amalia   Anastasia
Angela   Anna   Annunziata
Antonia   Antonietta   Arcangela
Argentina   Assunta   Aurora

Barbara   Bartolomea   Beatrice
Benedetta   Biaggia   Brunetta

Carmela   Carmina   Carolina

Cassandra   Catalda   Catarina
Cecilia   Celestina   Cesaria
Chiara   Concetta   Costanza
Cristina

Diana   Domenica   Dorotea

Elena   Elisabetta   Emanuella
Eufemia

Felicia   Filippa   Filomena
Flaminia   Francesca

Gabriela   Gaetana   Giacoma
Giovanna   Giudetta   Giulia
Giuseppa   Giuseppina   Grazia
Guida

Ignazia   Irena   Isabella

Laura   Laurizia   Leonarda
Letizia   Lorenza   Lucia
Lucrezia   Luiga   Luisa

Maddalena   Margherita   Maria
Mariangela Marianna   Marta
Michela

Nicola   Nicoletta   Nunzia

Oranza   Orsola   Ortenzia
Osvalda

Paola   Pasqua   Prudenza

Rachele   Raffaela   Regina
Romana   Rosa   Rosalia

Sabina   Santa   Saveria
Serafina   Sopia   Stefania

Teodora   Teresa

Valeria   Vincenza   Vita
Vittoria

Italian Letter-Writing Guide

The administrative details for writing to Italy for civil vital records and military records are provided in chapter nine. The addresses of the Italian archives are listed in Appendix C. This appendix assists in writing the actual letters. The necessary words, phrases and sentences are included here, which you may mix and match to create a custom letter. Substitute your own information for the *italicized words*. A sample completed letter is shown in figure B-1.

Greetings:

Dear Sirs	Egrègi Signori	
Dear Director	Egrègio Dircttóre	To an archive director
Dear Director	Gentile Direttrice	For a woman

Introductory sentences:

My name is *John Doe*.	Mi chiamo *John Doe*.
I live in the *United States*.	ito negli *Stati Uniti*.
I am trying to complete a history of my family.	Sóno alla ricérca della mia stòria familiare.
I am looking for information regarding my ancestors.	Cérco informazióni riguardo ai miei antenati.
I would like to find my relatives who remained in Italy.	Vorrei trovare I miei parènti rimasto in Italia.

Requests for Information:

I would appreciate if you could send me	Vi sarei grato se potètte spedirmi
the birth record	il atto di nàscita
the marriage record	il atto di matrimònio
the death record	il atto di mòrte
of my ancestor	del mio antenato
of my grandfather	del mio nònno
of my grandmother	della mia nònna
of my great-grandfather	del mio bisnònno

of my great-grandmother	della mia bisnònna	
of my great-great grandfather	del mio trisàvolo	
of my great-great grandmother	della mia trisàvola	
of my great-great-great grandfather	del mio quadrisàvolo	
of my great-great-great grandmother	della mia quadrisàvola	
Could you please have the conscription records for the province of *Bari* searched to find my ancestor?	Per favóre, potètte fare consultare le liste di lèva per la provìncia di *Bari*, e cercare il mio antenato?	Remember, military records are only available in the state archives (see chapter nine).
was born May 4, 1865	è nato il 4 maggio 1865	use *nata* for a female
was married May 4, 1865	è sposato il 4 maggio 1865	use *sposata* for a female
died on May 4, 1865	è morto il 4 maggio 1865	use *morta* for a female
was born in 1865	è nato nel 1865	use *nata* for a female
was born about 1865	è nato verso 1865	use *nata* for a female
was born between 1860 and 1865	è nato in mezzo di 1860 e 1865	use *nata* for a female
was born before 1865	è nato prima di 1865	use *nata* for a female
was born after 1865	è nato dopo di 1865	use *nata* for a female
emigrated to the United States in 1902	è emigrato negli Stati Uniti nel 1902	use *emigrata* for a female
in Naples	a Napoli	*ad* is used before a vowel
in Avellino	ad Avellino	
I know the following information about my ancestor:	Conósco I informazióni susseguènte a riguardo al mio antenato:	
the name of his/her father is	il nóme del suo padre è	
the name of his/her mother is	il nóme della sua madre è	
the name of his wife is	il nóme della sua móglie è	
the name of her husband is	il nóme del suo sposo è	
Could you please send the extract of this record?	Per favóre, potètte spedirmi il estratto di questo atto?	

Could you please send the entire record?	Per favóre, potette spedirmi il atto complèto?
Could you please send a photocopy, if possible?	Per favóre, potètte spedirmi una fotocòpia, se possìbile?
on non-legal paper	in carta lìbera
on legal paper	in carta legale
In the event that the information is not available, I ask that you send me a reply in the negative.	Nel caso che I informazióni non sìano disponìbile vi prègo di inviarmi una ripósta negativa.
Additionally, if the records do not exist for that period, or if you know of other sources, I would be grateful if you could suggest how my research could be pursued.	Inóltre, se I documénti non ci sóno per quél perìodo, o se Lei conósce altre fónti, Le sarei grata se potètte suggerirmi cóme proseguire la mia ricérca.

Payment Information

I ask you to charge me for the expense of the certificate.	Vi prègo di addebitarmi tutte le spése del certificato.
Enclosed is a cashier's check for *10,000* lire.	Qui incluso vi è un asségno per *10,000* lire.
I am enclosing two international reply coupons.	Inclùdo due tagliandi di postale universale.

Closing Sentences

I would be very thankful if you could provide this information.	Le sarei veramente grato se potètte provved érmi quest'informazióne.
Thank you kindly for your help.	Lei ringrazio gentilmente per il suo aiuto.
I send you my best regards.	Vi pòrgo I miei più distinti saluti.
Sincerely,	Cordialmente vòstro,
Best regards,	Distinti saluti,

For Follow Up Letters

I would like to thank you for your kindness in sending me information about my ancestors.	Vorrei ringraziarvi per la vòstra cortesia nell'inviarmi I informazióni dei miei antenati.

It has helped very much.	Ha aiutato moltisimo.
I would like to make another request.	Vorrei fare un'altra richièsta.
This is my second request to you without receiving your reply.	Questa è la seconda richièsta che le inriaro, non avèndo ricevuto una sua rispósta.
I fear that my previous letters have been lost or forgotten.	Tèmo che le mie lèttere precedènti sìano andate pèrse, o dimenticate.

Joseph Nano
123 Main Street
Anytown, NY 12345
U.S.A.

6 Settèmbre 1995

Ufficio di Stato Civile
Comune di Santa Maria Capua Vetere
81055 Santa Maria Capua Vetere (CE)
Italia

Egregi Signori,

Mi chiamo Joseph Nano ed abito negil Stati Uniti. Sóno alla ricérca della mis stòria familiare.

Vi sarei grato se poteste spedirmi il atto di nàscita del mio bisnònno, Antonio Nano. Antonio è nato a Santo Maria Capua Vetere verso 1890. Conosco i informazioni susseguente a reguardo al mio antenato:

Il nóme del suo padre è Vincenzo Nano. Il nóme della sua madre è Rosa (Rosaria) Lamberti.

Per favóre, potètte spedirmi il estratto di questo atto in carta lìbera? Vi prègo di addebitarmi tutte le spíse del certificato. Inclùdo due tagliandi di postale universale.

Le sarei veramente grato se potètte provvedérmi quest'informazióne. Lei ringrazio gentilmente per il suo aiuto.

Cordialmente vòstro,

Joseph Nano

FIGURE B-1 Sample letter.

Addresses of the Italian Archives

Archivio Di Stato Di Agrigento (e sezione di Sciacca)
Dir. Giuseppe Aurelio Giarrizzo
Via Mazzini, 187
92100 Agrigento—Italia (AG)
Tel. 0922/602494

Archivio Di Stato Di Alessandria
Dir. Nicola Vassllo
Via Solero, 43
15100 Alessandria—Italia (AL)
Tel. 0131/42794

Archivio Di Stato Di Ancona (e sezione di Fabriano)
Dir. Alessandro Mordenti
Via Maggini, 80
60127 Ancona—Italia (AN)
Tel. 071/2801840-2801841

Archivio Di Stato Di Arezzo
Dir. Augusto Antoniella
Via Albergotti, 1
52100 Arezzao—Italia (AN)
Tel. 0575/20803-354007

Archivio Di Stato Di Ascoli Piceno (e sezione di Fermo)
Dir. Carolina Ciaffardoni Ciarocchi
Via S. Serafino da Montegranaro 8/c
63100 Ascoli Piceno—Italia (AP)
Tel. 0141/531229

Archivio Di Stato Di Avellino
Dir. Andrea Sessa
Via S. Soldi, 9
83100 Avellino—Italia (AV)
Tel. 0825/36551

Archivio Di Stato Di Bari (e sezioni di Barletta e Trani)

Dir. Giuseppe Dibenedetto
Via L. Bissolati, 3
70125 Bari—Italia (BA)
Tel. 080/5024860

Archivio Di Stato Di Belluno
Dir. Giustiniana Migliardi O'Riordan
Via S. Maria dei Battuti, 3
32100 Belluno—Italia (BL)
Tel. 0437/940061

Archivio Di Stato Di Benevento
Dir. Elena Glielmo
Via dei Mulini, 148
82100 Benevento—Italia (BN)
Tel. 0824/21513

Archivio Di Stato Di Bergamo
Dir. Juanita Schiavini Trezzi
Via Tasso, 84
24100 Bergamo—Italia (BG)
Tel. 035/233131

Archivio Di Stato Di Bologna (e sezione di Imola)
Dir. Isabella Zanni Rosiello
Piazza Celestini, 4
40123 Bologna—Italia (BO)
Tel. 051/223891-239590

Archivio Di Stato Di Bolzano
Dir. Hubert Gasser
Via Armando Diza, 8
39100 Bolzano—Italia (BZ)
Tel. 0471/264295-264228

Archivio Di Stato Di Brescia
Dir. Luisa Bezzi
Via Galilei, 44
25124 Brescia—Italia (BS)
Tel. 030/305204

Archivio Di Stato Di Brindisi
    Dir. Marcella Guadulupi Pomes
    Piazza Santa Teresa, 4
    72100 Brindisi—Italia   (BR)
    Tel. 0831/523412

Archivio Di Stato Di Cagliari
    Dir. Marinella Ferrai Cocco Ortu
    Via Gallura, 2
    09125 Gagliari—Italia   (CL)
    Tel. 070/669450

Archivio Di Stato Di Caltanissetta
    Dir. Claudio Torrisi
    Via P. Borsellino, 2-2a
    93100 Caltanissetta—Italia   (CL)
    Tel. 0934/591600

Archivio Di Stato Di Campobasso
    Dir. Renata Pasquale de Benedettis
    Via Orefici, 43
    86100 Campobasso—Italia   (CB)
    Tel. 0874/90349

Archivio Di Stato Di Caserta
    Dir. Remo Stella
    Via Appia, 1 (loc. Torretta)
    81100 Caserta—Italia   (CE)
    Tel. 0823/355665

Archivio Di Stato Di Catania (e sezione di Caltagirone)
    Dir. Renata Maria Rizzo Pavone
    Via Vittorio Emanuele, 156
    95131 Catania—Italia   (CT)
    Tel. 095/7159860

Archivio Di Stato Di Catanzaro (e sezioni di Lamezia Terme e Vibo Valentia)
    Dir. Italo Montoro
    Piazza Rosario, 6
    88100 Catanzaro—Italia   (CZ)
    Tel. 0961/21446

Archivio Di Stato Di Chieti (e sezione di Lanciano)
    Dir. Carmine Viggiani
    Via F. Ferri, 27
    66100 Chieti—Italia   (CH)
    Tel. 0871/344032

Archivio Di Stato Di Como
    Dir. Vincenzo Intelligente
    Via Briantea, 8
    22100 Como—Italia   (CO)
    Tel. 031/306368

Archivio Di Stato Di Cosenza (e sezione di Castrovillari)
    Dir. Vittoria Cerulo Quarta
    Via Miceli, 67/71
    direz. via Panebianco
    87100 Cosenza—Italia   (CS)
    Tel. 0984/27201-392970

Archivio Di Stato Di Cremona
    Dir. Maria Luisa Corsi
    Via Antica Porta Tintoria, 2
    26100 Cremona—Italia   (CR)
    Tel. 0372/25463

Archivio Di Stato Di Cuneo
    Dir. Elia Vaira Caselli
    Via Monte Zovetto, 28
    12100 Cuneo—Italia   (CN)
    Tel. 0171/66645

Archivio Di Stato Di Enna
    Dir. Pietro Burgarella
    Via Scifitello, 20
    94100 Enna—Italia   (EN)
    Tel. 0935/37347

Archivio Di Stato Di Ferrara
    Dir. Giovanni Spedale
    Corso Giovecca, 146
    44100 Ferrara—Italia   (FE)
    Tel. 0532/206668

Archivio Di Stato Di Firenze (e sezione di Prato)
    Dir. Rosalia Manno Tolu
    Viale Giovane Italie, 6
    50122 Firenze—Italia   (FI)
    Tel. 055/2343554-2340875

Archivio Di Stato Di Foggia (e sezione di Lucera)
    Dir. Pasquale di Cicco
    Piazza XX settembre, 3
    71100 Foggia—Italia   (FG)
    Tel. 0881/621696-674019

Archivio Di Stato Di Forli (e sezioni di Cesena e Rimini)
Dir. Fiorenza Danti Mambelli
Via dei Gerolimini, 6
47100 Forli—Italia   (FO)
Tel. 0543/31217

Archivio Di Stato Di Frosinone (e sezione di Anagni-Guarcino)
Dir. Raffaele Santoro
Piazza De Mattheis, 41
03100 Frosinone—Italia   (FR)
Tel. 0775/872522

Archivio Di Stato Di Genova
Dir. Aldo Agosto
Via Tommaso Reggio, 14
16123 Genova—Italia   (GE)
tel. 010/293973

Archivio Di Stato Di Gorizia
Dir. Adele Brandi
Via dell'Ospitale, 2
34170 Gorizia—Italia   (GO)
Tel. 0481/535176-532105

Archivio Di Stato Di Grosseto
Dir. Serafina Bueti
Piazzi Socci, 3
58100 Grosseto—Italia   (GR)
Tel. 0564/26069

Archivio Di Stato Di Imperia (e sezioni di San Remo e Ventimiglia)
Dir. Francesca Fiandra Repetto
Via Matteotti, 105
18100 Imperia—Italia   (IM)
Tel. 0183/650491

Archivio Di Stato Di Isernia
Dir. Luigina Tiberio
Via L. Testa, 27
86170 Isernia—Italia   (IS)
Tel. 0865/26992

Archivio Di Stato Di L'Aquila (e sezione di Sulmona)
Dir. Gerado Miroballo
Piazza della Repubblica, 9

67100 L'Aquila—Italia   (AQ)
Tel. 0862/22501-27773

Archivio Di Stato Di La Spezia
Dir. Angelo Aromando
Via Galvani, 21
19100 La Spezia—Italia   (SP)
Tel. 0187/506360

Archivio Di Stato Di Latina
Dir. Eugenio Lo Sardo
Via dei Piceni, 24
04100 Latina—Italia   (LT)
Tel. 0773/610930

Archivio Di Stato Di Lecce
Dir. Chiara Piccolo
Via Sozy Carafa, 15
73100 Lecce—Italia   (LE)
Tel. 0832/246788

Archivio Di Stato Di Livorno
Dir. Paolo Castignoli
c/o palazzo del Governo
57100 Livorno—Italia   (LI)
Tel. 0586/897776-880028

Archivio Di Stato Di Livorno
Scali Cerere, 3
57122 Livorno—Italia   (LI)
Tel. 0586/880140

Archivio Di Stato Di Lucca
Dir. Giorgio Tori
Piazza Guidiccioni, 8
55100 Lucca—Italia   (LU)
Tel. 0583/491465

Archivio Di Stato Di Macerata (e sezione di Camerino)
Dir. Maria Grazia Pancaldi
Corso Cairoli, 175
62100 Macerata—Italia   (MC)
Tel. 0733/236521

Archivio Di Stato Di Mantova
Dir. Daniela Ferrari
Via Ardigò, 11
46100 Mantova—Italia   (MN)
Tel. 0376/324441-351243

Archivio Di Stato Di Massa (e sezione di Pontremoli)
Dir. Olga Raffo
Via G. Sforza, 3
54100 Massa—Italia (MS)
Tel. 0585/41684

Archivio Di Stato Di Matera
Dir. Antonella Manupelli
Via Tommaso Stigliani, 25
75100 Matera—Italia (MT)
Tel. 0835/331442

Archivio Di Stato Di Messina
Dir. Maria Intersimone Alibrandi
Via 24 maggio isol., 291
98100 Messina—Italia (ME)
Tel. 090/771006

Archivio Di Stato Di Milano
Dir. Gabriella Cagliari Poli
Via Senato, 10
20121 Milano—Italia (MI)
Tel. 02/76000369-76000282

Archivio Di Stato Di Modena
Dir. Angelo Spaggiari
Corso Cavour, 21
41100 Modena—Italia (MO)
Tel. 059/230549

Archivio Di Stato Di Napoli
Dir. Giulio Raimondi
Piazzetta Grande Archivio, 5
80138 Napoli—Italia (NA)
Tel. 081/204594-204491

Archivio Di Stato Di Novara (e sezione di Verbania)
Dir. Giovanni Silengo
Via dell'Archivio, 2
28100 Novara—Italia (NO)
Tel. 0321/398229

Archivio Di Stato Di Nuoro
Dir. Anna Lucia Segreti Tilocca
Via L. Oggiano, 22
Palazzo Ticca
08100 Nuoro—Italia (NU)
Tel. 0784/33476

Archivio Di Stato Di Oristano
Dir. Angelo Ammirati
Via G. Deledda
09170 Oristano—Italia (OR)
Tel. 0783/72092

Archivio Di Stato Di Padova (e sezione di Este)
Dir. Rita Baggio Collavo
Via dei Colli, 24
35143 Padova—Italia (PD)
Tel. 049/624146

Archivio Di Stato Di Palermo (e sezione di Termini Imerese)
Dir. Giuseppina Giordano
Corso Vittorio Emanuele, 31
90133 Palermo—Italia (PA)
Tel. 091/589693-589685

Piazzetta Gancia, 2
90139 Palermo—Italia (PA)
Tel. 091/6162772

Archivio Di Stato Di Parma
Dir. Marzio dall'Acqua
Via d'Azeglio, 45/e
43100 Parma—Italia (PR)
Tel. 0521/233185

Archivio Di Stato Di Pavia
Dir. Emanuela Salvione
Via Cardano, 45
27100 Pavia—Italia (PV)
Tel. 0382/539078

Archivio Di Stato Di Perugia (e sezioni di Assisi, Foligno, Gubbio, Spoleto)
Dir. Clara Cutini Zazzerini
Piazza G. Bruno, 10
06100 Perugia—Italia (PV)
Tel. 075/5731549-5724403

Archivio Di Stato Di Pesaro (e sezioni di Fano e Urbino)
Dir. Graziella Berretta
Via della Neviera, 44
61100 Pesaro—Italia (PE)
Tel. 0721/31851

Archivio Di Stato Di Pescara
Dir. Pasquale Damiani
Piazza della Marina, 2/4
65126 Pescara—Italia (PE)
Tel. 085/338521-64252

Archivio Di Stato Di Piacenza
Dir. Piero Castignoli
Piazza Cittadella, 29
Palazzo Farnese
29100 Piacenza—Italia (PC)
Tel. 0523/338521-385184

Archivio Di Stato Di Pisa
Dir. Giovanna Tanti
Lungarno Mediceo, 17
56100 Pisa—Italia (PI)
Tel. 050/542698-542784

Archivio Di Stato Di Pistoia (e sezione di Pescia)
Dir. Marina Laguzzi
Piazza Scuole Normali, 2
51100 Pistoia—Italia (PT)
Tel. 0573/23350

Archivio Di Stato Di Pordenone
Dir. Tullio Perfetti
Via Montereale, 7
33170 Pordenone—Italia (PN)
Tel. 0434/34356

Archivio Di Stato Di Potenza
Dir. Gregorio Angelini
Via Due Torri, 33 (sede provvisoria)
85100 Potenza—Italia (PZ)
Tel. 0971/411686

Archivio Di Stato Di Ragusa (e sezione di Modica)
Dir. Giovanni Morana
Viale del Fante, 7
97100 Ragusa—Italia (RG)
Tel. 0932/622200

Archivio Di Stato Di Ravenna (e sezione di Faenza)
Dir. Manuela Mantani
Via Guaccimanni, 51
48100 Ravenna—Italia (RA)
Tel. 0544/213674

Archivio Di Stato Di Reggio Calabria (e sezioni di Locri e Palmi)
Dir. Lia Domenica Baldissarro Di Pietro
Argine destro Annunziata, 59/61
89100 Reggio Calabria—Italia (RC)
Tel. 0965/22120

Archivio Di Stato Di Reggio Emilia
Dir. Gino Badini
Corso Cairoli, 6
42100 Reggio Emilia—Italia (RE)
Tel. 0522/4549211-451328

Archivio Di Stato Di Rieti
Dir. Roberto Marinelli
Viale Ludovico Canali, 7
02100 Rieti—Italia (FI)
Tel. 0746/204297

Archivio Di Stato Di Roma
Dir. Lucio Lume
Corso Rinascimento, 40
Palazzo della Sapienza
00186 Roma—Italia (RM)
Tel. 06/68803823-6872912

Archivio Di Stato Di Rovigo
Dir. Alberto Mario Rossi
Via Sichirollo, 9
45100 Rovigo—Italia (RO)
Tel. 0425/24051

Archivio Di Stato Di Salerno
Dir. Guido Ruggiero
Piazza Abate Conforti, 7
84100 Salerno—Italia (SA)
Tel. 089/225147

Archivio Di Stato Di Sassari
Dir. Anna Lucia Segreti Tilocca
Via G.M. Angioy, 1
07100 Sassari—Italia (SS)
Tel. 079/233470

Archivio Di Stato Di Savona
Dir. Guido Malandra
Via Quarda Superiore, 7
17100 Savona—Italia (SV)
Tel. 019/35227

Archivio Di Stato Di Siena
Dir. Sonia Adorni Fineschi
Via Banchi di Sotto, 52
53100 Sienna—Italia (SR)
Tel. 0577/41271-41101

Archivio Di Stato Di Siracusa (e sezione di Noto)
Dir. Salvatore Parisi
Via F. Crispi, 66
96100 Siracusa—Italia (SR)
Tel. 0931/22066

Archivio Di Stato Di Sondrio
Dir. Maristella La Rosa
Lungomallero Cadorna, 28
23100 Sondrio—Italia (SO)
Tel. 0342/514551

Archivio Di Stato Di Taranto
Dir. Ottavio Guida
Via di Palma, 4
74100 Taranto—Italia TA)
Tel. 099/4529413-4529412

Archivio Di Stato Di Teramo
Dir. Claudia Rita Castracane Vecchio
Via M. Delfico, 16
64100 Teramo—Italia (TE)
Tel. 0861/248893-240325

Circonvallazione Ragusa
64100 Teramo—Italia (TR)
Tel. 0861/243835

Archivio Di Stato Di Terni (e sezione di Orvieto)
Dir. Gigliola Fioravanti Fattorosi Barnaba
Vico del pozzo, 21
05100 Terni—Italia (TR)
Tel. 0744/425559

Archivio Di Stato Di Torino
Dir. Isabella Massabò Ricci
Sezione prima: piazzetta Mollino, 1
10124 Tornio—Italia (TO)
Tel. 011/5624431-540382

Sezione riunite: via S. Chiara, 40
10122 Tornio—Italia (TO)
Tel. 011/5211521-5211747

Archivio Di Stato Di Trapani
Dir. Santina Sambito
Via Libertá, 31
91100 Trapani—Italia (TP)
Tel. 0923/546355

Archivio Di Stato Di Trento
Dir. Salvatore Ortolani
Via Maccani, 161
38100 Trento—Italia (TN)
Tel. 0461/829008

Archivio Di Stato Di Treviso
Dir. Francesca Cavazzana Romanelli
Via A. Marchesan, 11/a
31100 Treviso—Italia (TV)
Tel. 0422/405517

Archivio Di Stato Di Trieste
Dir. Ugo Cova
Via La Marmora, 17
31139 Trieste—Italia (TS)
Tel. 040/390020-947251

Archivio Di Stato Di Udine
Dir. Ivonne Pastore Zenarola
Via Urbanis, 1
33100 Udine—Italia (UD)
Tel. 0432/477245

Archivio Di Stato Di Varese
Dir. Andreina Bazzi
Via Dol di Lana, 5
21100 Varese—Italia (VA)
Tel. 0332/312196

Archivio Di Stato Di Venezia
Dir. Paolo Selmi
Campo dei Frari, 3002
30125 Venezia—Italia (VE)
Tel. 041/5222281-5225406

Archivio Di Stato Di Vercelli (e sezioni di Biella e Varallo)
Dir. Maurizio Cassetti
Via Manzoni, 11
13100 Vercelli—Italia (VC)
Tel. 0161/64276-62525

Archivio Di Stato Di Verona
Dir. Angela Miciluzzo
Via Franceschine, 2/4
37122 Verona—Italia   (VR)
Tel. 045/8007639-8002713

Archivio Di Stato Di Vicenza (e sezione di Bassano del Grappa)
Dir. Giovanni Marcadella
Via Borgo Casale, 91
36100 Vicenza—Italia   (VI)
Tel. 0444/510827

Archivio Di Stato Di Viterbo
Dir. Alberto Porretti
Via M. Romiti
Localita' Le Pietrare
01100 Viterbo—Italia   (VT)
Tel. 0761/341023

Sezione Di Archivio Di Stato Di Anagni-Uarcino
Via del Monastero, 71
Palazzo Patrasso
03012 Agnagni-Guarcino—Italia   (FR)
Tel. 0775/46595

Sezione Di Archivio Di Stato Di Assisi
Vicolo degli Esposti, 6
06081 Assisi—Italia   (PG)
Tel. 075/816777

Sezione Di Archivio Di Stato Di Barletta
Via Ferdinando d'Aragona, 130
70051 Barletta—Italia   (BA)
Tel. 0883/331002

Sezione Di Archivio Di Stato Di Bassano Del Grappa
Via Beata Giovanna, 58
36031 Bassano del Grappa—Italia   (VI)
Tel. 0424/24890

Sezione Di Archivio Di Stato Di Biella
Piazza Cisterna, 9
Palazzo dal Pozzo della Cisterna
13051 Biella—Italia   (VC) (BI)
Tel. 015/2522294

Sezione Di Archivio Di Stato Di Caltagirone
Via ex Matrice, 153

95041 Caltagirone—Italia   (CT)
Tel. 0933/26380

Sezione Di Archivio Di Stato Di Camerino
Via Venanzi, 20
62032 Camerino—Italia   (MC)
Tel. 0737/3052

Sezione Di Archivio Di Stato Di Castrovillari
Via Santa Maria del Castello
87012 Castrovillari—Italia   (CS)
Tel. 0981/21141

Sezione Di Archivio Di Stato Di Cesena
Via Montalti, 6
47023 Cesena—Italia   (FO)
Tel. 0547/610754

Sezione Di Archivio Di Stato Di Este
35042 Este—Italia   (PD)
Tel. 049/624146

Sezione Di Archivio Di Stato Di Fabriano
Via C. Battisti, 23
60044 Fabriano—Italia   (AN)
Tel. 0732/3127

Sezione Di Archivio Di Stato Di Faenza
Via Manfredi, 14
48018 Faenza—Italia   (RA)
Tel. 0546/21808

Sezione Di Archivio Di Stato Di Fano
Via Castracane, 3
61032 Fano—Italia   (PS)
Tel. 0721/8012129

Sezione Di Archivio Di Stato Di Fermo
Via G. Leopardi, 2
63023 Fermo—Italia   (AP)
Tel. 0734/228739

Sezione Di Archivio Di Stato Di Foligno
Piazza Repubblica
06034 Foligno—Italia   (PG)
Tel. 075/9271593

Sezione Di Archivio Di Stato Di Gubbio
Via Oderigi Lucarelli
Palazzo Ducale

06024 Gubbio—Italia   (PG)
Tel. 075/9271593

Sezione Di Archivio Di Stato Di Imola
Via Verdi, 6
40026 Imola—Italia   (BO)
Tel. 0542/30316

Sezione Di Archivio Di Stato Di Terme
Via XX settembre, 68
Palazzo Bilotti
88046 Lamezia Terme—Italia   (CZ)
Tel. 0968/22048

Sezione Di Archivio Di Stato Di Lanciano
Viale Cappuccini, 131
66034 Lanciano—Italia   (CH)
Tel. 0872/49424

Sezione Di Archivio Di Stato Di Locri
Via Matteotti, 302
89044 Locri—Italia   (RC)
Tel. 0964/22163

Sezione Di Archivio Di Stato Di Lucera
Via dei Saraceni, 1
71036 Lucera—Italia   (FG)
Tel. 0881/841219-941219

Sezione Di Archivio Di Stato Di Modica
Via Liceo Convitto, 35
97015 Modica—Italia   (RG)
Tel. 0932/941252

Sezione Di Archivio Di Stato Di Noto
Via Amerigo Vespucci, 30
96017 Noto—Italia   (SR)
Tel. 0931/838569

Sezione Di Archivio Di Stato Di Orvieto
Piazza del Duomo, 31
05018 Orvieto—Italia   (TR)
Tel. 0763/43415

Sezione Di Archivio Di Stato Di Palmi
Via Carbone, 3
89015 Palmi—Italia   (RC)
Tel. 0966/411230

Sezione Di Archivio Di Stato Di Pescia
Viale Europa, 7

51017 Pescia—Italia   (PT)
Tel. 0572/477261

Sezione Di Archivio Di Stato Di Pontremoli
Via Nazionale
Ex convento SS. Annunziata
54027 Pontremoli—Italia   (MS)
Tel. 0587/831559

Sezione Di Archivio Di Stato Di Prato
Via Lapo Mazzei, 41
50047 Prato—Italia   (FI) (PO)
Tel. 0574/26064

Sezione Di Archivio Di Stato Di Rimini
Via C. Cattaneo, 2
47037 Rimini—Italia   (FO) (RN)
Tel. 0541/21688

Sezione Di Archivio Di Stato Di Remo
Corso Cavallotti, 362
18038 San Remo—Italia   (IM)
Tel. 0184/508910

Sezione Di Archivio Di Stato Di Sciacca
Via Giuseppe Verdi, 27
92019 Sciacca—Italia   (AG)
Tel. 0925/24896

Sezione Di Archivio Di Stato Di Spoleto
Piazza interna delle Mura, 1
06049 Spoleto—Italia   (PG)
Tel. 0743/43789

Sezione Di Archivio Di Stato Di Sulmona
Via S. Cosimo, 16
67039 Sulmona—Italia   (AQ)
Tel. 0864/31690

Sezione Di Archivio Di Stato Di Termini Imerese
Via Cannolo, 1
90018 Termini Imerese—Italia   (PA)
Tel. 091/8143789

Sezione Di Archivio Di Stato Di Trani
Via Dogali, 11
70059 Trani—Italia   (BA)
Tel. 0883/583522

Sezione Di Archivio Di Stato Di Urbino
Via Veneto, 42

61029 Urbino—Italia (PS)
Tel. 0722/2621

Sezione Di Archivio Di Stato Di Varallo
Via Tancredi Rossi, 9
13019 Varallo—Italia (VC)
Tel. 0163/51234

Sezione Di Archivio Di Stato Di Ventimiglia
Via Hanbury, 12
18039 Ventimiglia—Italia (IM)
Tel. 0184/34855

Sezione Di Archivio Di Stato Di Verbania
Via Cadorna, 37
28048 Verbania—Italia (NO) (VB)
Tel. 0323/501403

Sezione Di Archivio Di Stato Di Vibo Valentia
Viale della Pace
Palazzo de Fina
88018 Vibo Valentia—Italia (CZ) (VV)
Tel. 0963/45613

Research Forms

This appendix contains useful forms for your research. You may make copies of them for your own use. Sample completed forms are included throughout the book. There are two basic types of forms included, the Italian Genealogy Research Checklist and several Data Extract Forms.

Italian Genealogy Research Checklist

This form (figure D-1) lists the steps, in sequence, to follow for a specific research task. Use one form for each task; for example, to find the birth record of your great-great-grandmother. This form is especially useful when researching more than one ancestor at a time because it helps you organize and track your progress. Sample completed Italian Genealogy Research Checklists are included in chapter ten as part of a case study. The tasks on each section of this form are discussed in detail in the following sections of this book:

I. Establish a Goal—see chapter three.
II. Determine Document Location—see chapter nine.
III. Perform the Research—chapters six, seven and eight cover how to use the records.

Data Extract Forms

To assist you in transcribing the information that you find in the records of the *Stato Civile,* use these Data Extract Forms. There are forms for birth records (figure D-2), marriage records (figure D-3) and death records (figure D-4). Even if you make photocopies of the original microfilmed records, you should still fill out these forms. Sometimes photocopies are not very clear and you may need to refer back to your original transcription. These forms contain places for all the genealogical information that may be available in the civil vital records of the *Stato Civile.* Not all the records you find will contain all the information shown on these forms. Just fill in the appropriate blanks. If you find information in the original record for which there is no appropriate space, use the Miscellaneous Notes space.

When filling out these Data Extract Forms, always enter the information exactly as it appears in the original record, in Italian. For example, if a person's age is listed as *trentadue* (32), write out *trentadue,* not 32. If you try to translate as you transcribe, you may make an error, for example, write *23* instead of *32.* To avoid this possibility, always write the exact, original information. If you like, write the translation in parentheses after the original phrase.

Sample completed Data Extract Forms are included throughout this book wherever an original birth, marriage or death record appears (chapters eight and ten).

Italian Geneology Research
Checklist

I. Establish a Goal

        Who: _____

        What: _____

        Where: _____

        When: _____

II. Determine Document Location

        A. First, check the Family History Library

            1. check the FHL catalog for the town's records

            2. Determine microfilm number:_____

            3. Order film. Date ordered: _____

            4. Film has arrived. Date due: _____

        B. If not available in Family History Library

            1. Write letter to Italy

III. Perform Research

        A. Review microfilm

            1. Find required year

            2. Find index for year

            3. Search index for ancestor

            4. Find document

            5. Complete data extraction form for document

            6. Photocopy document

            7. Update research log to record successful or unsuccesful research

            8. Review all the indices on microfilm for surnames

            9. Make note of siblings and relatives

            10. Update your research log to record the names for which you searched

        B. Or Review Extract from Italy

            1. Update your research log to record success or failure.

IV. What Have I Learned

        A. List new information discovered in this research process

	Ancestor	Ancestor	Ancestor	Ancestor
Who:				
What:				
Where:				
When:				
Misc.:				

V. Fill Out New Research Checklists for Above Goals

FIGURE D-1 **Italian Genealogy Research Checklist Form.**

Data Extract Form

Stato Civile of Italy—Birth Record of: _____

Document Source

| Microfilm: | Title: |
| Year: | Document Number: |

Record Creation

| Date: |
| Clerk: |
| Place: |

Informant

Name:	Age:
Birthplace:	Son/Dau of:
Occupation:	Residence:

Parents

	Mother	Father
Name:		
Birthplace:		
Age:		
Dau/Son of:		
Occupation:		
Residence:		
Notes:		

Child

| Name: |
| Birthdate: |
| Baptism Info: |
| Notes: |

Witnesses

	Witness 1	Witness 2
Name:		
Birthplace:		
Age:		
Son/Dau of:		
Occupation:		
Residence:		

Margin Notations

Miscellaneous Notes

Researcher: _____ Date: _____

FIGURE D-2 **Data Extract Form for birth records.**

Data Extract Form

Stato Civile of Italy—Marriage Record of: _____

and: _____

Document Source

Microfilm:	Title:
Year:	Document Number:

Record Creation

Date:
Clerk:
Place:

Marriage Date:

	Groom	Bride
Name:		
Birthplace:		
Age:		
Occupation:		
Residence:		
Notes:		
Father:		
Occupation:		
Residence:		
Mother:		
Occupation:		
Residence:		

Witnesses

	Witness 1	Witness 2
Name:		
Birthplace:		
Age:		
Son/Dau of:		
Occupation:		
Residence:		

	Witness 3	Witness 4
Name:		
Birthplace:		
Age:		
Son/Dau of:		
Occupation:		
Residence:		

Miscellaneous Notes

Researcher: _____   Date: _____

FIGURE D-3 **Data Extract Form for marriage records.**

Data Extract Form

Stato Civile of Italy—Death Record of: _____

_____

Document Source

Microfilm:	Title:
Year:	Document Number:

Record Creation

Date:
Clerk:
Place:

Informant

	Informant 1	Informant 2
Name:		
Birthplace:		
Age:		
Son/Dau of:		
Occupation:		
Residence:		

Deceased

Name:	
Death Date:	
Place of Death:	
Birthplace:	
Age:	
Occupation:	
Residence:	
Father:	
Occupation:	
Residence:	
Mother:	
Occupation:	
Residence:	

Witnesses

	Witness 1	Witness 2
Name:		
Birthplace:		
Age:		
Son/Dau of:		
Occupation:		
Residence:		

Miscellaneous Notes

Researcher: _____ Date: _____

FIGURE D-4 **Data Extract Form for death records.**

BIBLIOGRAPHY

Allen, Morton. *Morton Allan Directory of European passenger steamship arrivals for the years 1890 to 1930 at the Port of New York and for the years 1904 to 1926 at the ports of New York, Philadelphia, Boston, and Baltimore.* Baltimore, Maryland: Genealogical Publishing Co., Inc., 1987.

Center for Migration Studies, *Piety and Power: The Role of Italian Parishes in the New York Metropolitan Area, 1880 - 1930.* New York: Center for Migration Studies, 1975.

Cole, Trafford R. *Italian Genealogical Records: How to use Italian Civil, Ecclesiastical, and Other Records in Family History Research.* Salt Lake City, Utah: Ancestry Incorporated, 1995.

Coletta, John P. *Finding Italian Roots.* Baltimore, Maryland: Genealogical Publishing Co., Inc., 1993.

————. *They Came in Ships: A Guide to Finding Your Immigrant Ancestor's Arrival Record.* Salt Lake City, UT: Ancestry Incorporated, 1993.

Cordasco, Francesco. *Dictionary of American Immigration History.* Metuchen, New Jersey: Scarecrow Press, 1990.

Daniels, Roger. *Coming to America; A History of Immigration and Ethnicity in American Life.* New York: HarperPerennial, 1990.

Dollarhide, William. *Managing a Genealogical Project.* Baltimore, Maryland: Genealogical Publishing Co. Inc., 1993.

Filby, P. William, ed. *Passenger and Immigration Lists Bibliography, 1538 - 1900.* Detroit, Michigan: Gale Research, 1988.

————. *Passenger and Immigration Lists Index: A Guide to Published Arrival Records of about 500,000 Passengers who Came to the United States and Canada in the Seventeenth, Eighteenth and Nineteenth Centuries.* Detroit, MI: Gale Research, 1993.

Foerster, Robert F. *The Italian Emigration of our Times.* New York: Arno Press, 1969.

Fucilla, Joseph G. *Our Italian Surnames.* Baltimore, Maryland: Genealogical Publishing Co., Inc., 1993.

Glazier, Ira A. and P. William Filby, eds. *Italians to America: Lists of Passengers Arriving as U.S. Ports, 1880 - 1899.* Wilmington, Delaware: Scholarly Resources, 1993.

Hall, Marie Ets. *Rosa, The Life of an Italian Immigrant.* Minneapolis, Minnesota: University of Minnesota Press, 1970.

Iorizzo, Luciano J. and Salvatore Mondello. *The Italian Americans.* Boston: Twayne Publishers, 1980.

Jacobus, Donald L. *Genealogy as Pastime and Profession.* Baltimore, Maryland: Genealogical Publishing Co. Inc., 1991.

Stella, Antonio. *Some Aspects of Italian Immigration to the United States.* New York: G.P. Putnam and Sons, 1924.

Stratton, Eugene Aubrey. *Applied Genealogy.* Salt Lake City, Utah: Ancestry, Inc., 1988.

Trease, Geoffrey. *The Italian Story: From the Etruscans to Modern Times.* New York, Vanguard Press, 1963.

U.S. Department of Commerce. *Historical Statistics of the United States.* Washington, DC: Bureau of the Census, 1975.

INDEX

A

Abbreviations
   given names, 40
   in the vital records, 40-41
   months, 40
   provinces, 87
Addresses of Italian archives, 128-136
Allegati, 57, 75
Alphabet, Italian, 37
Altamura, Bari, Apulia, 47
Altavilla, 23
Ancestral File, 30
Annexed documents, 57, 75
Applied Genealogy, 9
Archives, Italian State, 85, 86, 128-136
Archives, National, 26, 27, 28, 30, 31
Archivio di Stato, 85, 86, 128-136
Atto di matrimonio. *See* Marriage records
Atto di Morte (death record), 75-80, 85, 106
   index, 47-49
Atto di nascita (birth record), 53-57, 58-61, 85, 101, 109-112
   index, 44, 45, 101
Atto di notificazione, 57, 62-66
Atto di pubblicazione, 57, 62-66
Atto di solenne promessa di matrimonio. *See* Marriage records

B

Baltimore, 28
Bari, Bari, Apulia, 12, 47, 53
Birth records, 53-57, 58-61, 85, 101, 109-112
   index, 44, 45, 101
Boston, 28, 29
Bureau of Immigration and Naturalization, 27, 28

C

Capital cities, provincial, 15
Carta legale, 88
Carta libera, 88
Caserta, Caserta, Campania, 2, 22
Cavour, 11
Census records, 26
Church of Jesus Christ of Latter-day Saints, The, 30, 81
Citizenship, Italian, 114
Cluster genealogy, 7
Colloquialisms, 41
Comuni
   description, 12
   how to find, 22
Confirming information, 9
Correspondence, 85-88, 123-127

D

Data extract forms, 96, 137
   blank
      birth, 139
      death, 141
      marriage, 140
   example
      birth, 61, 112
      death, 80
      marriage, 74, 104
   using, 96, 137
Databases, genealogical, 30-31
   Ancestral File, 30
   GenServ, 30
   IGI, 30
   POINT, 30-31
Dates, 40, 42, 43-44
Death records, 75-80, 85, 106
   index, 47-49
Deceased, terms for, 41
Declaration of Intention, 27
Determining your immigrant ancestor's hometown, 22-32
Di, 41
Dictionary, Italian/English, using, 51-52
Document examples
   birth record, 53-57, 58-61, 101, 109-112
   birth record index, 44, 45, 101
   death record, 75-80
   death record index, 47-49
   marriage record, 66-74, 96-100
   marriage record index, 44, 46, 47, 92, 95
   wedding banns, 62-66
Document formats, 4-5

E

Elba, Livorno, Tuscany, 12

F

Family History Center, 5, 31, 35, 81-82
Family History Library, 5, 26, 30, 31, 32, 35, 81, 85
Family History Library Catalog, 82, 84-85, 90, 96
First names
   abbreviations, 40
   examples, 121-122
Four W's, 7, 18, 90, 96
Frazioni
   description, 12
   how to find, 22
Fu, 41

G

Gazetteers, Italian, 31
Gender distinction
    in grammar, 42
    of babies, 53-54
Genealogical databases, 30-31
    Ancestral File, 30
    GenServ, 30
    IGI, 30
    POINT, 30-31
Genealogies, published, 31
Genealogy as a Pastime and Profession, 9
GenServ, 30
Geographical organization of Italy, 12
Given names
    abbreviations, 40
    examples, 121-122
Goals, 7
Gravina di Puglia, Bari, Apulia, 47, 82, 85, 90, 96, 101
Grimaldi, Cosenza, Calabria, 12

H

Handwriting, 34, 37-40
History of Italy, 10-12

I

Idioms, 41
IGI, 30
Immigration
    name changes, 23-25
    North American resources, 23-30
    numbers by year, 23
    ports of arrival, 28
    to North America, 22
    to the United States by region, 24
Indices
    Italian vital records, 35, 43-49
        birth records, 44, 45, 101
        death records, 47-49
        marriage records, 44, 46, 47, 92, 96
        reference numbers, 43
Indices, ships' passenger lists, 28
International Genealogical Index, 30
International reply coupons, 86
IRC. *See* International reply coupons
Italian citizenship, 114
Italian English dictionary, 51
Italian gazetteers, 31
Italian Genealogical Group of New York, 115
Italian Genealogical Records: How to use Italian Civil, Ecclesiastical, and Other Records in Family History Research, 115-116
Italian genealogical resources, 31-32
    gazetteers, 31

military records, 31-32
    surname books, 32
Italian Genealogical Society of America, 115
Italian Genealogy Research Checklist, 90, 91, 96, 105, 137, 138
Italian military records, 31-32, 86
Italian naming traditions, 18
Italian State Archives, 85, 86, 128-136
Italians in Chicago: a Study of Americanization, The, 31
Italians to America: Lists of Passengers Arriving at U.S. Ports, 1880-1899, 28-29
Italian surname books, 32
Italian word lists, 117-122
    cardinal numbers, 117
    days of the week, 117
    first names, female, 122
    first names, male, 121-122
    general genealogical terms, 118
    months, 118
    occupations, 120-121

J

Julian calendar, 40

L

Language barrier, 34
LDS, 30, 81
Leading Americans of Italian Descent in Massachusetts, 31
Lecce, 23
Legal paper, 88
Letter writing guide, 123-127
Library of Congress, 31, 114
Lire, payment in, 87-88

M

Maiden names, 29, 36
Managing a Genealogical Project, 9
Maps
    modern Italy, 15
    obtaining, 114
    provinces, 17
Margin notations, 35-36, 49-51
Marriage banns, 57, 62-66
Marriage records, 57, 62, 66-74, 85, 92, 96-100, 102-104
    allegati, 57, 75
    atto di matrimonio, 66-74
    index, 44, 46, 47, 92, 95
    notificazioni, 57, 62-66
    processetti, 57, 75
    pubblicazioni, 57, 62-66
    wedding banns, 57, 62-66
Military records, Italian, 31-32, 86
Months
    abbreviations, 40
    list of, 118
Mormons, 30, 81

Morton-Allen Directory of European Passenger Steamship Arrivals, 29

N

Name changes
    provinces, 12
    surnames, 23-25
Names, first
    abbreviations, 40
    examples, 121-122
Names, given
    abbreviations, 40
    examples, 121-122
Naming traditions, 18
Napoleon, 10-11, 35
National Archives, 26, 27, 28, 30, 31
Naturalization, 26
New Orleans, 28
New York, 26, 27, 28, 29
Nineteenth-century society, 19-20
North American genealogical resources
    Primary sources, 23-30
        census records, 26
        description, 25
        naturalization documents, 27
        passport applications, 29-30
        ships' passenger lists, 27-29
    primary versus secondary, 25
    Secondary sources, 25, 30-31
        genealogical databases, 30-31
            Ancestral File, 30
            GenServ, 30
            IGI, 30
            POINT, 30-31
        published genealogies, 31
Notificazioni, 57, 62-66
Numbers
    abbreviations, 40
    cardinal, 117
    handwritten examples, 39
    ordinal, 117
    written, 42
Nuovo dizionario dei comuni e frazioni di comuni con le circonscizioni amministrative, 31

O

Occupations, list of common, 120-121
Our Italian Surnames, 32
Overview, 4

P

Paleography, 34, 37-40
Palo del Colle, Bari, Apulia, 47, 82
Passenger and Immigration Lists Bibliography, 1538 - 1900, 28
Passports, 29-30

Peasant, typical day, 20
Philadelphia, 28
Phone books, 32
POINT, 30-31, 115
Pre-unification names of provinces, 13
Primary sources, North American, 23-30
    census records, 26
    description, 25
    naturalization documents, 27
    passport applications, 29-30
    ships' passenger lists, 27-29
Processetti, 57, 62-66
Procura della Repubblica, 85
Provinces
    abbreviations, 87
    capital cities, 15
    description, 12
    list of, 16
    map, 17
    military districts, 32
    name changes, 12
    pre-unification, 13
Pubblicazioni, 57, 62-66
Published genealogies, 31
Pursuing Our Italian Names Together, 30-31, 115

R

Record keeping, 8
Redundancy, 51
Regioni. *See* Regions
Regions
    description, 12
    list of, 16
    map, 15
Registri degli Uffici di Leva, 31-32, 86
Registri di Leva, 31-32, 86
Research forms, 137-141
Research process, 4
    summary steps, 5
Risorgimento, 11
Ruesch International, 88
Rutigliano, 2

S

Sample documents
    birth record, 53-57, 58-61, 101, 109-112
    birth record index, 44, 45, 101
    death record, 75-80
    death record index, 47-49
    marriage record, 66-74, 96-100
    marriage record index, 44, 46, 47, 92, 95
    wedding banns, 62-66
San Pietro, 2
Santa Maria di Capua Vetere, Caserta, Campania, 31
Santeramo, Bari, Apulia, 47

Secondary sources, North American, 25, 30-31
   genealogical databases, 30-31
      Ancestral File, 30
      GenServ, 30
      IGI, 30
      POINT, 30-31
   published genealogies, 31
Ship photographs, 114
Ships' Passengers Lists, 27-29
   customs lists, 28
   immigration lists, 28
   indices, 28
Social classes, 19
Society, nineteenth-century, 19-20
State Archives, Italian, 85, 86, 128-136
Stato Civile (vital records), 34, 85
   advantages, 35-36
   birth records, 53-57, 58-61, 85, 101, 109-112
   consistency, 35
   death records, 75-80, 85, 106
   disadvantages, 34-35
   indices, 35, 43-49
   margin notation, 35-36, 49-51
   marriage records, 57, 62, 66-74, 85, 92, 96-100, 102-104
      allegati, 57, 75
      atto di matrimonio, 66-74
      index, 44, 46, 47, 92, 95
      notificazioni, 57, 62-66
      processetti, 57, 75
      pubblicazioni, 57, 62-66
      wedding banns, 57, 62-66
   offices of, 85
Steamship Historical Society of America, 114
Surname books, Italian, 32
Surname changes, 23-25

T
Time formats, 42
Titles, 40, 42
Towns
   descriptions, 12
   how to find, 22

U
Ufficio di Stato Civile, 85-86
Undecipherable records, 34-35
Unification of Italy, 10-12
Unpuzzling Your Past, 9
Using an Italian/English dictionary, 51

V
Victor Emmanual II, 11
Vital records, 34, 85
   advantages, 35-36
   birth records, 53-57, 58-61, 85, 101, 109-112
   consistency, 35
   death records, 75-80, 85, 106
   disadvantages, 34-35
   indices, 35, 43-49
   margin notation, 35-36, 49-51
   marriage records, 57, 62, 66-74, 85, 92, 96-100, 102-104
      allegati, 57, 75
      atto di matrimonio, 66-74
      index, 44, 46, 47, 92, 95
      notificazioni, 57, 62-66
      processetti, 57, 75
      pubblicazioni, 57, 62-66
      wedding banns, 57, 62-66
   offices of, 85
Vital Records, initiation by Napoleon, 11

W
Wedding banns, 57, 62-66
Word continuations, 41
Word lists, Italian, 117-122
   cardinal numbers, 117
   days of the week, 117
   first names, female, 122
   first names, male, 121-122
   general genealogical terms, 118
   months, 118
   occupations, 120-121
Work Projects Administration, 28
WPA, 28
Writing to Italy, 85-88, 123-127

More Great Books Full of Great Ideas!

A Genealogist's Guide to Discovering Your African-American Ancestors—Uncover your ancestry with this one-of-a-kind guide that addresses the all-important questions such as how to begin, defining goals, resources needed to start your search and more! *#70369/$16.99/128 pages/22 b&w illus./paperback*

Family Memories—Take your family memories from the shoe box to the showcase! This vibrant book contains hundreds of ideas and patterns for creating beautiful family albums in rememberance of any occasion. You'll also discover creative ways to feature special photos, while protecting them from fading and deterioration. *#70389/$21.99/128 pages/150 color, 90 b&w illus./paperback*

Paper Pizazz Series—Preserve cherished memories with these paperback books full of 64 acid-free, full-color sheets perfect for memory albums or scrapbooks! You'll learn new ways to display your photos and keepsakes on pages complete with spaces for journal entries and clippings.

> **Family Scrapbook Paper Pizazz**— *#70390/$16.99/128 pages*

> **Holiday Scrapbook Paper Pizazz**— *#70391/$16.99/128 pages*

Reaching Back—Record your life's most meaningful moments to share with future generations. This easy-to-use keepsake edition includes space for family stories, important documents, recipes, photos, heirlooms, family trees and more. *#70360/$14.99/160 pages/paperback*

Family History Logbook—Now you can weave your personal histories into the colorful web of national events using these historical happenings spanning the years 1900 to 2000. You'll have plenty of room to record your own milestones—from dates and events to interviews with relatives. *#70345/$16.99/224 pages/paperback*

The Unpuzzling Your Past Workbook: Essential Forms and Letters for All Genealogists—Now unpuzzling your past is easier than ever using 42 genealogical forms designed to make organizing, searching, record-keeping and presenting information effortless. *#70327/$15.99/320 pages/paperback*

Unpuzzling Your Past: A Basic Guide to Genealogy, 3rd Edition—Make uncovering your roots easy with this complete genealogical research guide. You'll find everything you need—handy forms, sample letters and worksheets, census extraction forms, a comprehensive resource section, bibliographies and case studies. Plus, updated information on researching courthouse records, federal government resources and computers on genealogy. *#70301/$14.99/176 pages/paperback*

The Genealogist's Companion & Sourcebook—Discover promising primary and secondary sources! You'll learn how to get past common obstacles and how to use cluster genealogy effectively. Plus, you'll learn about such information sources as church and funeral home records, government documents, court records, newspapers and maps. Also included are bibliographies, case studies, census forms, a family group sheet and information on major archives, libraries, lending libraries and publishers. *#70235/$16.99/256 pages/paperback*

Writing Family Histories and Memoirs—From conducting solid research to writing a compelling book, this guide will help you recreate your past. Polking will help you determine what type of book to write, why you are writing the book and what its scope should be. Plus, you'll find writing samples, memory triggers and more! *#70295/$14.99/272 pages/paperback*

Families Writing—Here is a book that details why and how to record words that go straight to the heart—the simple, vital words that will speak to those you care most about and to their descendants many years from now. *#10294/$14.99/198 pages/paperback*

How to Write the Story of Your Life—Leave a record of your life for generations to come! This book makes memoir writing an enjoyable undertaking—even if you have little or no writing experience. Spiced with plenty of encouragement to keep you moving your story towards completion. *#10132/$13.99/230 pages/paperback*

Writing From Personal Experience—There was that moment—a poignant truth, a lesson learned—that turned your life around. Now you can share your story with the help of this inspiring and instructive guide, complete with nuts-and-bolts instruction—from getting your story down on paper to getting it out to editors. *#10510/$16.99/208 pages*

Writing Personal Essays: How to Shape Your Life Experiences for the Page—Discover how to put your life story on paper. You'll learn how to choose just the right personal-experience topic and how to build a story loaded with emotion and significance. Bender offers inspiration to help you every step of the way. *#10438/$17.99/272 pages*

Writing Articles From the Heart: How to Write & Sell Your Life Experiences—Holmes gives you heartfelt advice and inspiration on how to get your personal essay onto the page. You'll discover how to craft a story to meet your needs and those of your readers. *#10352/$16.99/176 pages*

Making Books by Hand—Discover 12 illustrated, step-by-step projects for making handmade albums, scrapbooks, journals and more. You'll learn basic techniques, as well as creative binding and decorating alterations you can use to make each of your books unique. Only everyday items like cardboard, wrapping paper and ribbon are needed. *#30942/$24.99/108 pages/250 color illus.*

Conquering the Paper Pile-Up—Now there's hope for even the messiest record keeper! You'll discover how to sort, organize, file and store every piece of paper in your office and home. Plus, you'll get instruction on how to deal with life's most important documents! *#10178/$11.95/176 pages/paperback*

Stephanie Culp's 12-Month Organizer and Project Planner—The projects you're burning to start or yearning to finish will zoom toward accomplishment by using these forms, "To-Do" lists, checklists and calendars. Culp helps you break any project into manageable segments, set deadlines, establish plans and follow them—step by attainable step. *#70274/$12.99/192 pages/paperback*

Streamlining Your Life—Tired of the fast-track life? Stephanie Culp comes to the rescue with quick, practical, good-humored and helpful solutions to life's biggest problem—not having enough time. You'll get practical solutions to recurring problems, plus a 5-point plan to help you take care of tedious tasks. *#10238/$11.99/142 pages/paperback*

Slow Down and Get More Done—Discover precisely the right pace for your life by gaining control of worry, making possibilities instead of plans and learning the value of doing "nothing." *#70183/$12.99/192 pages/paperback*

How to Have a 48-Hour Day—Get more done and have more fun as you double what you can do in a day! Aslett reveals reasons to be more productive everywhere—and what "production" actually is. You'll learn how to keep accomplishing despite setbacks, ways to boost effectiveness, the things that help your productivity and much more. *#70339/$12.99/160 pages/120 illus./paperback*

Make Your House Do the Housework, Revised Edition—Take advantage of new work-saving products, materials and approaches to make your house keep itself in order. You'll discover page after page of practical, environmentally friendly new ideas and methods for minimizing home cleaning and maintenance. This book includes charts that rate materials and equipment. Plus, you'll find suggestions for approaching everything from simple do-it-yourself projects to remodeling jobs of all sizes. *#70293/$14.99/208 pages/215 b&w illus./paperback*

Don't Be A Slave to Housework—Discover how to get your house in order and keep it that way. You'll learn to arrange a schedule to get your housework done, get your spouse in on the housekeeping action, unclutter your home, do preventative maintenance, use more brain power than elbow grease to clean and much more! *#70273/$10.99/176 pages/paperback*

Don Aslett's Clutter-Free! Finally and Forever—Free yourself of unnecessary stuff that chokes your home and clogs your life! If you feel owned by your belongings, you'll discover incredible excuses people use for allowing clutter, how to beat the "no-time" excuse, how to determine what's junk, how to prevent recluttering and much more! *#70306/$12.99/224 pages/50 illus./paperback*

You Can Find More Time for Yourself Every Day—Professionals, working mothers, college students—if you're in a hurry, you need this time-saving guide! Quizzes, tests and charts will show you how to make the most of your minutes! *#70258/$12.99/208 pages/paperback*

Confessions of a Happily Organized Family—Deniece Schofield shows you how to work as a family to restore—or establish for the first time—a comfortable sense of order to your home. You'll find specific organizational techniques for making mornings and bedtimes more peaceful, making chores fun, storing kids' stuff and much more! *#01145/$10.99/248 pages/paperback*

Clutter's Last Stand—You think you're organized, yet closets bulge around you. Get out of clutter denial with loads of practical advice. *#01122/$11.99/280 pages/paperback*

The Organization Map—You *will* defeat disorganization. This effective guide is chock full of tips for time-management, storage solutions and more! *#70224/$12.99/208 pages/paperback*

Office Clutter Cure—Discover how to clear out office clutter—overflowing "in" boxes, messy desks and bulging filing cabinets. Don Aslett offers a cure for every kind of office clutter that hinders productivity—even mental clutter like gossip and office politics. *#70296/$9.99/192 pages/175 illus./paperback*

Is There Life After Housework?—All you need to take the dread out of housework are some ingenious ideas and a little

inspiration. You'll find both in Aslett's revolutionary approach designed to free you from the drudgery of housework! *#10292/$10.99/216 pages/paperback*

It's Here . . . Somewhere—Need help getting and keeping your busy household in order? This book provides step-by-step instruction on how to get more places out of spaces with a room-by-room approach to organization. *#10214/$10.99/192 pages/50 b&w illus./paperback*

How To Conquer Clutter—Think of this book as a "first aid guide" for when you wake up and find that clutter has once again taken over every inch of available space you have. You'll get insightful hints from A to Z on how to free yourself from clutter's grasp. *#10119/$11.99/184 pages/paperback*

How to Get Organized When You Don't Have the Time—You keep meaning to organize the closet and clean out the garage, but who has the time? Culp combines proven time-management principles with practical ideas to help you clean-up key trouble spots in a hurry. *#01354/$11.99/216 pages/paperback*

Confessions of an Organized Homemaker—You'll find hundreds of tips and ideas for organizing your household in this totally revised and updated edition. Discover motivation builders, consumer product information and more! *#70240/$10.99/224 pages/paperback*

Cleaning Up for a Living, 2nd Edition—Learn from the best! Don Aslett shares with you the tricks and tips he used to build a $12 million commercial cleaning business. *#70016/$16.99/208 pages/paperback*

Holiday Fun Year-Round With Dian Thomas—A year-round collection of festive crafts and recipes to make virtually every holiday a special and memorable event. You'll find exciting ideas that turn mere holiday observances into opportunities to exercise imagination and turn the festivity all the way up—from creative Christmas gift-giving to a super Super Bowl party. *#70300/$19.99/144 pages/paperback*

Friends & Lovers: How to Meet the People You Want to Meet—Discover how to turn your favorite activities into a personal action plan for meeting people! *#01294/$13.99/202 pages/paperback*

Step-by Step-Parenting—Learn the secrets to strong bonds among families created out of second marriages. This inspirational guide covers everything from the games step-children play to a step-parent's rights. *#70202/$12.99/224 pages/paperback*

The Big Wedding on a Small Budget Planner & Organizer—Plan an elegant wedding without sending your family to the poorhouse. This handy planner offers budget guidelines, plenty of detailed worksheets and ample space for notes and cost comparisons. *#10322/$12.99/128 pages/paperback*

Roughing It Easy—Have fun in the great outdoors with these ingenious tips! You'll learn what equipment to take, how to plan, set up a campsite, build a fire, backpack—even how to camp during winter. *#70260/$14.99/256 pages/paperback*

Into the Mouths of Babes: A Natural Food Nutrition and Feeding Guide for Infants and Toddlers—Discover 175 economical, easy-to-make, vitamin-packed, preservative-free recipes. Plus, you'll find a shopper's guide to whole foods, methods to cope with allergies, a comprehensive prenatal and infant nutrition resource and what not to put into the mouths of babes! *#70276/$9.99/176 pages/paperback*

The Single Person's Guide to Buying A Home: Why to Do It and How to Do It—This buying guide offers you worksheets and checklists that show you what to look for when buying a home on your own. *#70200/$14.95/144 pages/paperback*

How to Start Making Money With Your Crafts—Launch a rewarding crafts business with this guide that starts with the basics—from creating marketable products to setting the right prices—and explores all the exciting possibilities. End-of-chapter quizzes, worksheets, ideas and lessons learned by successful crafters are included to increase your learning curve. *#70302/$18.99/176 pages/35 b&w illus./paperback*

Speaking With Confidence: A Guidebook for Public Speakers—Tips and exercises show you how to overcome stage fright and improve your speaking abilities. *#70101/$9.95/176 pages/paperback*

Cover Letters That Will Get You the Job You Want—Discover how to introduce yourself and your resume compellingly and efficiently with a well-written, well-constructed cover letter. Includes 100 tested cover letters that work! *#70185/$12.99/192 pages/paperback*

The Selling-From-Home Sourcebook: A Guide to Home-Based Business Opportunities in the Selling Industry—Work from home, meet people and make money at the same time! With this unique reference, you'll learn to define your goals as you explore a wealth of advice on setting up your own home-based sales business. You'll also discover a world of information about careers in sales, plus listings of over 100 companies that offer home-based selling opportunities. *#70316/$17.99/272 pages/paperback*

Interview Strategies That Will Get You the Job You Want—Stand out from the crowd when meeting prospective employers! Key takes you from preparation through the interview process as you learn how to get invited to the interview, present yourself professionally, ask the right questions, avoid damaging slips of the lip and many other essentials. *#70314/$12.99/144 pages/paperback*

The Complete Guide to Building and Outfitting an Office in Your Home—You'll discover how to convert basements and attics, determine space needs, create layouts—even specifics like how to keep house sounds out! *#70244/$18.99/176 pages/105 b&w illus./paperback*

Export-Import: Everything You & Your Company Need to Know to Compete in World Markets, Revised Edition—Get the vocabulary, insider tips and rules of the game you need to compete in rapidly expanding world markets. This revised edition will help you stay on top of the competition with the latest information on trade laws and government regulations including those for NAFTA and GATT. *#70285/$16.99/160 pages/paperback*

Mortgage Loans: What's Right for You? 4th Edition—Don't make a big-money mistake signing for the wrong mortgage! Find the facts on the types of mortgages perfectly suited to your needs and financial situation. Plus, get information on caps, margins, points and more! *#70336/$14.99/144 pages/paperback*

The Complete Guide to Buying Your First Home—This information-packed guide shows you how to plan and organize your buy and how to avoid common pitfalls for first-time home buyers. *#70023/$16.99/224 pages/paperback*

Creative Kitchen Decorating—Beautify your kitchen—or create an all-new one—with this recipe book of fabulous design and decorating ideas. Vivid color photographs and clear explanations cover everything from lighting and layout to storage and work surfaces, plus much more! *#70322/$16.99/128 pages/250+ color illus./paperback*